T0114984

The DEAFENING CADENCE *of* BIBLICAL DEFECTION

Can Christianity survive in an anti-Christian America?

ROBERT DELICH, PH.D.

WESTBOW
PRESS
A DIVISION OF THOMAS NELSON

WestBow Press books may be ordered through booksellers or by contacting:

WestBow Press
A Division of Thomas Nelson
1663 Liberty Drive
Bloomington, IN 47403
www.westbowpress.com
1-(866) 928-1240

Because of the dynamic nature of the Internet, any web addresses or
links contained in this book may have changed since publication and
may no longer be valid. The views expressed in this work are solely those
of the author and do not necessarily reflect the views of the publisher,
and the publisher hereby disclaims any responsibility for them.

Any people depicted in stock imagery provided by Thinkstock are models,
and such images are being used for illustrative purposes only.

Certain stock imagery © Thinkstock.

ISBN: 978-1-4497-6058-8 (sc)
ISBN: 978-1-4497-6060-1 (hc)
ISBN: 978-1-4497-6059-5 (e)

Library of Congress Control Number: 2012913152

Printed in the United States of America

WestBow Press rev. date: 08/03/2012

Acknowledgments

I dedicate this book to all my Christian friends and family members in Christ but most of all to those who literally gave and to those who continue to give their life defending America and the Biblical oracles of Jesus Christ free from political and denominational influence.

Table of Contents

About This Book

This book is more than a revelation of personal encounter. It is a collection of selected historical trials and tribulations that emphasize what it means to live and suffer as a Christian. More importantly, it is an evidenced reflection of what happens to the moral construct of a nation when it turns its back on God. This weltering reality is made clear without the aid of impetuous doctrine implored by any specific Christian denomination. Instead, each chapter is a true to life account surrounding some of the most troublesome historicity of the Christian church all the way up to the more recent menacing tentacles of the anti-Christian movement in America. Of particular mention are the biased, leftist media; inaccurate, political propaganda from the film industry; the selling of militant humanism in our schools; political correctness; and a liberal court system that finds it appropriate to assist and legitimize scriptural abominations into law. Showing little regard for the Word of God, these anti-Christian agencies have become a menacing parasitic force, tearing at the very fabric of Christian ideology and the moral stability of America. The question is what kind of country will we assign to the next generation if man's self-serving, immoral inequities are the measuring tool that represents final authority? In addition to the moral collapse, and unprecedented economic hardship, at no time in the history of America is Christianity fighting for its life. In so many ways this fight can be traced to the very thin line that separates an agitating-liberal-Democratic style of government from that of tyranny. With this said, aside from the signing of the Declaration of Independence, the election of 2012 will be the most important election in the history of America.

Surfacing in a variety of ways, the courts and orchestrated militant humanism in our public school system represents the strictest element of anti-Christian agenda in America, but other parts of the world experience a more radical approach. Churches are burned, and Christians are randomly slaughtered in some of the most brutal ways. The studies of such atrocities are certainly not for the faint of heart. Moreover, formulating and promoting intellectual and political hypotheses to justify such inhumane practices is not cause to celebrate, especially since rationalization has little to do with scriptural truths that hold men accountable and tethered to civility.

Although each chapter outlines a specific theme, one inescapable question remains self-evident. What do provocateurs of anti-Christian God sentiment and Christian infighting expect to gain from such a repugnant agenda? Realistically, this is a difficult question to answer in such a limited space, but it would be accurate to say three leading causal variables are government power and control, denominational dominance, and liberal reformation of civil law to accommodate those of a lesser moral standard. True in every sense of the word, nonetheless, most important to this work is the unmitigated stance and presentation of the one true God as delineated throughout the Old and New Testament. It is by this method that understanding and resolutions for conceptual issues in this book emerge.

Although the relevance of this model is most appreciated in the discussions about the struggle for religious dominance, Christians should refrain from doctrinal bickering because this is time away from the real issues at hand. By and large, one issue in particular is the failure to be in consort with what to do about the ill-hearted logic of the immoral, selfish spoilers who demands social recognition for their perversities. Left to itself, the anti-biblical God movement is strengthened, and the poignancy of scriptural disdain for abominations is weakened. A lack of Christian unified resolve also allows the court's ability to sanction repugnant abominations under the guise of equal civil rights. Though I am not perfect, I do have the capacity to see when something negative is moving against the grain of normalcy, especially where immoral incivilities can find safety in deliberate and reckless judicial prudence that affects the moral heart of the country. By overstepping moral and legal boundaries, modern-day courts have become the extended version of the Sanhedrin's killing of Christ, but in a different way. I view this statement as credibly accurate because without the teachings of Jesus Christ, there would be no one to challenge the priestly Sadducee interpretation of the Law. More importantly, who would bring salvation and grace to the people certainly not the undeveloped, unmoral conscience of a self-monitored people.

Religion and its importance relative to moral civility cannot be underestimated because without question, recent history shows that because America is abandoning the religious ideals and social laws that contributed to its greatness, we are witnessing an obvious pattern for its demise. For example, the mantra of "In God We Trust" was once paramount, but the anti-Christian and anti-Semitic idiosyncrasies, along with nationwide disdain for the indefatigable a priori truths of the Father, Son, and Holy Spirit, are now openly blasphemed by anti-God leftists, atheists, and those professing that there are other ways to heaven.

Contributing to this blasphemy is Christian replacement theology and various destructive biblical critics who seek to either humiliate or disprove the idea of a Christian God. Scripture is quite clear about consequences for nations who turn their backs on God or look to change the words of His book: "The wicked shall be turned into hell, and all nations that forget God"[1]; "For the nation and kingdom that will not serve thee shall perish; yea those nations shall be utterly wasted"[2]; and most importantly, "And if any man shall take away from the words of this prophecy, God shall take away his part out of the Book of Life, and out of the holy city, and from the things which are written in this book."[3] Rest assured, the rash of fires, floods, drought, the economic downturn, the waters running dirty, and the immoral direction of our nation are not coincidental. If America does not return to God, this is only the beginning, and the worst is to come. President Regan said it best, "If we ever forget we are a nation under God, then we will be a nation gone under."

Should I be surprised that rebellion against long-standing Christian traditions would come from those of a leftist political view? Not hardly. Dedicated to opposing the very thing Christian doctrine is built upon, the intimate connection between leftist open disdain for Christianity is as obvious as the devotees of evolution traveling to Darwin's "holy land", the Galapagos Islands. Protected under constitutional right to voice open denigration of Christian symbolism and its doctrines, conversely, the hypocrisy and fullness of leftist thinking and political correctness does not allow one to speak ill of Islamic Jihad or refer to radical Islam as terrorism. In fact, political correctness has gone as far as to eliminate from school textbooks by whom and why the twin towers were viciously destroyed. In textbooks across America, there is no mention of radical Islam, Osama bin Laden, or that 9-11 was part of Islamic Jihad. The youth of today are being taught and influenced by leftist inaccurate presentation and elimination of the facts. Ironically, the pitfalls of the democratic process lend itself to protecting such politically adverse groups. Conversely, the eminent danger of protecting such distortion lies in the fact that America's survival depends on what our leaders do, think, and believe and will determine what kind of nation America will become. Also, within the leftist arsenal, it is okay for God to be circumvented, and the joy of immorality, coupled with scandalous economic and political cover-up, is revered. At what point will these immoral infractions cease? From a Christian perspective, the book supports the idea that this degradation can only get worse because civil courts are now in the empirical business of supporting and protecting those of an anti-Christian maleficent heart. Hence, "Every kingdom divided against itself is brought to desolation; and every city or house divided against itself shall not stand."[4] The one saving grace from government's self-imposed exceptive sovereignty is that the third Temple will be built and Christ will return.

Aside from the cited anti-Christian organizations, the book also points out how biblical defection is hardly one-dimensional. Precisely, the deterioration of spiritual guidance within traditional family structure, the onslaught of macabre and sexually perverted media, children having children, children born out of wedlock, infidelity, drugs, incest, and an educational system polluted by leftist anti-God and anti-American criterion each contribute to the destruction of the morality and integrity of the United States. Much to blame for the growth of this immoral road is a disgraceful, corrupt, and faltering political and religious leadership that has breached its role as protector of social and moral equilibrium. Yes, Christians do fall, and in the wake of this failure, the Engle vs. Vitale case of 1962 and Madelyn Murray O'Hair's subsequent push to eliminate school prayer has caused two generations to lapse into what scarcely resembles conscionable morality. Thus, it only stands to reason that to satisfy the whims of a select few, governmental and judicial appeasement has greatly contributed to altering the moral conscience of America. Had the squeaky wheel not been attended, the issue of school prayer probably never would have been addressed. The ramifications of this transformation are many, but none is greater than how it affects the youth of America. "While the Bible, the principal foundational book of America's documents, is banned from public schools in America, in Islamic countries the Quran is taught in the school systems the moment the child can read. Muslims are aware that in order to win the next generation, it begins with the youth."[5] In every respect, parents need to have an in-depth conversation with their children before culture does.

What do these spiritual and political transgressions mean for a country whose history has received much of its strength from investments in the oracles of Scripture? Because we have lost our passion for a righteous God, court-approved, unconscionable, sinful acts have replaced the essential soundness of moral decency. Comparatively, the immoral decadence and fate of Sodom and Gomorrah and the obvious decline of America's social and moral structure are already Babylonian. Unfortunately, only the believers can see this analogous truth. Contributing to this inheritance are the liberal left-wing advocacy attorneys and organizations that defend against citizenry disapproval of certain immoral lifestyles. They are the very same legalists that condemn and fight against the true Christian believers, endeavoring to save social and moral principalities from extinction. Living without God's guidance and help, America cannot survive. In fact, one of the saddest days in America was the elimination of prayer from schools. It is also my opinion that the early introduction of sex education merely aroused emotions and helped to seduce and encourage active participation rather than curtail behavior. These two elements mark the beginning of the end for maintaining and exhibiting a national moral conscience.

In summary, the purpose of this book is to point out how the unambiguous depth and range of lengthy Christian bickering, court-ordered leftist thinking, and interference by a discombobulated self-serving government have greatly contributed to shaping the decadent sociopolitical anti-Christian God reality and social breakdown we have come to know and accept. Directly, the course of these actions has made America a morally troubled nation where the masses accept right as wrong and wrong as right. God is mocked, leaders in every category are openly corrupt, mediocrity is acceptable, and expressing truth has become a crime. If ever, these immoral insurrections won't be going away any time soon, and in many ways they have been the inspiration for this work. The question is, at what point do Christians as a whole say enough is enough? What will it take for the discriminate Christian believer to realize that the future for applied Christian doctrine will largely be determined on how united Christians remain in the effort to cauterize any future doctrinal concessions brought on by the anti-Christian movement? In more ways than one, the deafening cadence of bible defection is a legitimate and urgent call for concern and I am fully prepared to absorb the subsequent criticism for choosing to dine with the truth.

Introduction

A prerequisite for acknowledging this work as a reasonable representation of accurate and truthful evidentiary precepts is embracing the proposition that time as we know it began with the Old Testament creation story of Adam and Eve. Otherwise the contents could not be held as Christian truths against any of the collective opposing referenced arguments discussed within. This is especially true in that there is only one truth, and that truth dictates that you cannot stand for and against that truth at the same time. In the words of Norman L. Geisler, "God made the rules, it is simply our duty to keep them and leave the results in His hands."[1] Another important detail to ponder is the idea whether or not you are easily offended and entrenched in believing that your Christian denomination is the only way to Christ. This would be a good time to stop reading because denominational prejudice and replacement theology is a major contributor to many of Christendom's problems. More importantly, we must never forget that clergy are men and women first, and they harbor the same lust and characterological deficits as everyday citizens. Precisely, death and God's judgment are not things that happen only to ordinary people. In fact, Paul, the most revered advocate for Christ, demonstrated and admitted to his poor judgment in many of his dealings with the public and some of the chosen disciples.

Objectivity is important when reading this book, because the harsh reality of the referenced biblical truths within these covers strongly supports the position that there are no civil court orders or known amendments, modifications, or asterisks tied to Scriptural truths. Subsequently, scientific explanations, exclusionary pardons, or justifications for blasphemy and immoral lifestyles do not exist. These acts all fall under the heading of abominations. Quite frankly, personal judgment and preferential ideals can best be served when rummaging through the tomatoes at the supermarket but not when it comes to the exactitudes of God's Word. Reinventing His Word to accommodate an immoral religious, political, personal, or social agenda is blasphemous. If God condoned such behaviors he would have made provision for them in the greatest book ever written. What Jesus did give us is His warning not to disrupt the cornerstone of His written Word: "For I testify unto every man that heareth the words of the prophecy of this book, if any man shall add unto these things, God shall add unto him the plagues that are written in this book."[2] This warning includes changing words of Scripture to appease or accommodate the doctrine of another religion: "To whom then will ye liken me, or shall I be equal? saith the Holy One."[3]

Reading through the various chapters, you will realize that the Christian persecutions of today are no different from any of the previous inhumane atrocities and doctrinal attacks that punctuate Christian history. Shamefully, many of these persecutions have their roots in Christian infighting. Modern-day examples of this particular aspect of Christian history are the book's presentation of the long-standing, unresolved doctrinal issues between Eastern Catholic Orthodoxy and Western Roman Catholicism, much of which openly resurfaced during the Bosnian War.

In consort with today's multifaceted anti-Christian sentiment, no Biblical defense is ever complete without a discussion on the absolutes of creation truths versus the ongoing saga of pro-Darwin evolutionary science. Of the many threats to Christian doctrine, selling evolution as the origin of man is one of the most damaging movements because the Genesis creation story necessitates a belief in a divine creator. Negating this principle would imply there is no God, thereby creating a mythological impetus for all the players and incidences in scriptural history.

Alluding to the torchbearers for Darwinism, we also find a select group of scientific intellectuals who go as far as to say that a physical God does not exist. This belief in itself red flags the credibility of anti-God studies and makes sensible dialogue with these models virtually impossible. What more proof does one need than the fulfillment of over 600 biblical prophecies, with the most transcendent being the return of the Jews to Israel? In fact, at the time of the writing of this book we are witnessing the road to fulfilling Isaiah 17, which prophesizes the fall and destruction of Damascus, and Isaiah 19, which prophesizes Egyptians against Egyptians. These biblical prophecies are divinely sanctioned by the One who delivers all that He promises. Relativistically, when it comes to God's truths, a hypothetical world has no defense against the reality of Jesus' promises. Even as such, there still are counterclaims to the reality of His second coming. The second coming I speak of is that of Jesus Christ and has nothing to do with Obama's bid for a second term in the White House. But by all accounts of biblical prophecy, the inflexible blasphemous non-believers who look to create a different America will soon find themselves in an extremely compromised position.

Governed by the constructs and proclamations of a Christian conscience, included is a chapter on the ethical issues relative to abortion, euthanasia, artificial insemination, and other controversial issues whose fate was presented to and decided by the courts. One in particular is the controversial civil court ruling that in some states "lawfully" protect the Trojan horse of same-sex marriage. Although only a few states recognize this civil ruling, preservation of morality cannot survive if civil courts stay in the business of legislating across-the-board protection for immorality. By its own decisions, I believe the court should be labeled an oxymoron because legalizing immorality is contrary to the moral operational semantics of the court itself. With the pendulum swinging so far to the left, the unanchored youthful and impressionable minds, whose strengths and weaknesses are continuously tested by the onslaught of immoral crusades, are at risk. Three such crusades are educational sex curriculum in schools, easy access to birth control, and the idea that it's okay to have homosexual parents. This is exactly why the integral part of this work is unmistakably geared toward the importance of employing a Christian conscience when making moral-based decisions, something the courts and our nation's leaders have been lacking in for quite some time.

Before going any further I would like to make it clear that my position on Biblical abominations and anti-Christian sentiment are not predicated on hate. I speak from a disciplined Christian perspective, which I choose not to relinquish just to accommodate someone else's preferred behavior that may be contrary to my Christian beliefs. But for a civil court to force a valetudinarian agenda on a nation whose historical roots are legally articled as Christian, I cannot remain silent. Furthermore, just because the court supports abominations does not mean that I, as a Christian, should be legally bound or forced to abandon God's law as prescribed by my Christian belief. God's law and civil law are two mutually exclusive concepts. In fact, this is the same dilemma that confronted Christians when they were expected to bow down to Roman paganism. Literally, choosing the God of Abraham, while living in a land that enforced sin through national civil law, had to be difficult. But the choice was clear paganism or death, and many chose death. Although we have not reached this point in America, predatory courts utilize a different approach. Anti-Christian doctrine is enforced through civil law, which translates to telling Christians we have no choice. This puts Christians in a position of having to accept blasphemy; so much for separation of church and state. As a result, parents find themselves having to protect their children from immoral influences imposed by the court's redefinition of moral boundaries. The effects of court decisions and government's involvement in the reconstruction of society have caused the loss of two generations to an unconscionable psychological profile without boundaries. This has all materialized because government is now in the business of legislating immorality. Furthermore, we have a president who is not shy about demonstrating a lackluster position for those symbolic representations of anything Christian. An example of this was evidenced when the White House requested that the symbol for Christ, IHS, be covered over during Obama's speech at Georgetown University in April 2008. Defenders of this act would prefer to have you believe that this request needs to be put in its proper perspective. I say no to this because the source of this request and approval had to come from the president. Something is dramatically amiss when a Jesuit, Catholic university allowed this to happen. I also contend that those in positions of governmental power and leftist organizations have knowingly taken the liberty to transgress on the "national everything" that has worked for over two-hundred years. It is only the believers that can see how anti-Christian movements and governments' efforts to rid the connection between man and traditional historic Christianity has done nothing but validate and fuel the fallen nature of mankind. Consequently, "To whom then, will ye liken God? Or what likeness will ye compare unto Him?"[4]

Granted, with a court order comes the technical documentation that itemizes stipulations of a law. Civil law, however, has absolutely nothing to do with the moral conscience of a Christian who subscribes to the transcriptions of God's law as presented in Scripture. This is especially true since politicians and judges like to remind us of policy guidelines relative to the separation of church and state.

In matters contrary to God's law, God's law stands as supreme law and the social functional significance of certain anti-Christian behavioral patterns approved by the court do not automatically preclude or lower a practicing Christian's threshold for tolerance. In particular and in the eyes of a devoted Christian who believes in and lives by the Holy Sacraments of Scriptural context, homosexuality and same-sex marriages will always be an abomination no matter what the court or legislature decides because choosing between morality and immorality is not a legislative issue. Deuteronomy, Leviticus, and Romans are adamant about their warnings and pitfalls concerning these particular behavioral transgressions, and the floods, fire, drought, tornados, and ten year period of economic downturn are living proof of God's reprimand when He is displeased. Yes, I do believe these are the beginning stages of God's wrath. Furthermore, if the United States continues to bargain for Middle East peace using Israel's land and God's capital, Jerusalem, as a bargaining chip, the worse is yet to come. This is God' city, and under no circumstances will He relinquish ownership because, "For the Lord hath chosen Zion; He hath desired it for His habitation."[5] In addition, "when the Jews re-formed Israel in 1948, reunited Jerusalem as the capital in 1967, and annexed their original Promised Land with the 1948 Israeli boundaries, God restored His promise to Abraham and David. [So] when a world leader demands a division of the land, he or she is actually coming against the covenant that God sealed with His own name!"[6]

When dealing with the controversial contemporary issues of our deteriorating society, overly exuberant courts have gotten ahead of themselves by assuming the power of civil law can ultimately change the heart of a true practicing Christian's viewpoint on biblical abominations. Christians have long established their position on such matters, and unlike the courts, Christians do not have to force Christianity on anyone because it is written that there is a time and place for everything. Besides, when Jesus said, "No man comes to the Father but by Me," He meant that nothing happens until the Father ordains it. Yes, I do believe America's crumbling is God ordained and because we have turned our back on God, God will bring America to its knees. Essentially, it all boils down to leadership and choice, and if a non-recipient of Christ does not believe that "thou shall pay all debts," the only thing left for that individual is "death by the wages of sin" with right and wrong choices being the academic explanation for sin. Foremost, to the exclusion of all else, no one gets away with anything, and as Scripture dictates, the sins of the parents, leaders included, will ultimately fall upon the heads of their children.

As the court uses its legal authority to malevolently force sinful abominations on all of America's citizenry, this forced agenda loses its implied affectivity with practicing Christians. It is presumptuous to even think a chosen immoral way of life can genuinely fit in with those who by biblical law are committed to opposing abominable behavior and mannerisms. Liberals like to use such conviction to have you believe that Christians and conservatives demonize people. But the truth of the matter is, people demonize themselves. Furthermore, to deprive true Christians of their allegiance to the laws of one true God is nothing but revisiting forced Roman paganism.

In consideration for whatever side of this argument one lives, it is foolish to think it is possible to escape the biblical premise that, "The Lord is our judge, the Lord is the Lawgiver, the Lord is our King; He will save us."[7] Wanting to rein over the world, Satan is working and manipulating his way into defying every Scriptural page of God's teaching and influence, which in many ways accounts for the crumbling of the United States from within. Likewise, for a court or national leader to knowingly make or approve laws that hurt a righteous populous, this can only come from a heart that is self-serving and indebted to the antichrist movement. "Woe unto them that decree unrighteous decrees and that write grievousness which they have prescribed."[8]

Among other issues, chapter one gives a brief discussion on the origin of man from a Christian perspective weighted against evolutionary science. I say brief because the divergences on this controversial saga are far too voluminous and beyond the practical intent for this book. In any event, of the many battles that challenge Christian doctrine, this is one battle the Christian community cannot afford to lose because evolutionary science and its theoretical precepts, along with socialist propaganda, are fast becoming the determinate as to what is taught in educational systems. This is a dangerous precedent because it shields those individuals who have not had the opportunity to consider coming to Christ; lest we forget that in a dictatorship, religion and Christ are constrained or, in many cases, virtually nonexistent.

To remedy this dangerously immoral dimension of scientific teaching, rather than wait for the proverbial "they" to take action, it is the duty of every Christian to stave off this creeping darkness. Personal responsibility is the key, and unless Jesus Himself intervenes, there is no other way. Unfortunately, people as a whole tend to put more trust in the deception and lies of a presidential candidate who promises hope and change rather than the words of Jesus Christ, the God who delivers what He promises. Preoccupied by the latest electronic gadgets, the general population has become mentally sterile and is oblivious to the real truth behind governmental propaganda. Addicted to I-Pods, fun and circus, like sheep they willingly go to slaughter.

The remaining chapters of this book are layered in open discussions on Jesus' role in the preservation of mankind, the future for a Biblical conscience, and whether Christianity can survive in America, let alone the world. I have to ask this question because even with the current state of worldwide anti-Christian and anti-Semitic sentiment, rather than calling it the Holy War that radical Islam makes reference too, euphemisms in political and religious arenas avoid labeling atrocities against Christians as such. Europe and the Middle East have experienced a dramatic increase of blatant brutal assaults on those who profess Christianity, but the most devastating assault was the modern-day slaughter of thousands of Christians by radical Muslims in Southern Sudan in the early 1990s. For untold reasons, the press shied away from calling this butchery a religious war and referred to it as tribal warfare. Call it what you may, but the raw implications of these worldwide assaults are already far beyond the label of "tribal warfare." In fact, at the time of writing this book, tens of thousands of Roman Catholic Sudanese are being forced to leave Northern Sudan by radical Islamists. The irony is that the world is sensitive to these incursions, but the potential explosiveness of it all is what keeps the political lid on taking an offensive stance toward the known provocateurs. Case in point, Kosovo always was and technically still belongs to Serbia, but it is my opinion that because of oil and the threat of increased terrorism, the United States and the world chose to appease Islam.

The book purposely starts with the Biblical beginning because the beginning is the starting point for living proof on how far the pendulum has swung for the worse. As stated earlier, seemingly judicious in their rulings but highly incompatible with Judeo-Christian doctrine, civil courts have indiscriminately passed final judgment on moral issues without fully understanding the severity of their legal prescriptions and the long-term effects of unnatural behavioral patterns forced on the many by and for a select few. These types of rulings are socially and politically dangerous and do little to support the birthed hallmarks given by the forefathers or the meandering, exploratory youth of this and future generations. Furthermore, who would know better than our political "leaders" that morality cannot be legislated? "For as many as have sinned without law shall also perish without law: and as many as have sinned in the law shall be judged by the law."[9]

While addressing the needs of various lobbyist groups, the aim, supposedly, is to ensure equality for everyone. Although this gesture looks nice on paper, the practicality of equality is not possible. In order for equality to serve equally, It must represent exactly that; equal in every respect otherwise "equality" is nothing more than an euphemistic pacifying trade-off to accommodate one of many festering social issues in the overcooked and faltering democratic "pie-in-the-sky melting pot." Furthermore, when a politician advocates for equality at all levels, the word equality itself becomes an oxymoron. Equality at all levels is virtually impossible because a politician's ultimate goal is to separate themselves as far as they can from the serfs who put him in office. Subsequently, addressing the equality issue through courts or legislation is nothing but a concocted lie and a political crumb-throwing gesture to keep the masses civil.

Deceptive in more ways than one, the battle cry for equality may as well include the heresy that biblical expectations are far too stringent and archaic in their application of moral, civil, and religious law, which is why courts need to intervene to protect "democratic" civil rights for everyone. To the contrary, biblical prescriptions, especially in early biblical times, were upheld by God-fearing, zealous people who were determined to live by the oracles of God to avoid experiencing the wrath of God. History shows that the human spirit of the founding fathers of America also savored a reverence for God. As an appreciation for the gifts from God, the word God was used in some of the very constitutional and ideological prescriptions that outline the founding of this great country. But today America has been overrun by a different animal, a leftist political machine impregnated with hypocrisy and living off the fat of the land, while at the same time working to ensure its demise. It's ironic that America condemns other nations for such practices. But only in America and without reprisal can those who dishonor Judeo-Christian religion mock, slander, burn, spit on, and denigrate the holiest book of the Judeo-Christian faith.

Plainly, a disregard for a fear of God has made our nation a liberal and egocentric society far detached from the Judeo-Christian Biblical value system that once was revered as our nation's universal strength and norm for upholding human decency and accountability. Now, Christians against their will are subjected to a court-ordered, across-the-board alternate lifestyle standard for moral decency. Historically, military men in skirts have been tried before but ultimately contributed to dethroning those nations as a worldly power. Equally damaging are the educational institutions that preach evolution and deep leftist anti-God ideals to young and impressionable minds. The implications of imposing such dramatic change lead me to believe global respect is in jeopardy, as well as the future of the moral and physical preparedness of our nation.

If this seems too critically far-fetched, take a good look at what has happened to the integrity and morality of the House of Representatives and the U.S. presidential office. There was a time when the president was viewed as a role model. But, the past 25 years has proven to be otherwise. The danger of this slow but steady abandonment of integrity, ethics, and Christian principles by elected leadership is an ominous warning of the world to come. Was it not Confucius who said "How leaders behave, the people will follow?" In every practical sense of the word, we are past the doorstep of Isaiah 3:12: "As for my people, children are their oppressors, and women rule over them, O my people, they which lead thee cause thee to err, and destroy the way of thy paths."[10]

Without a doubt, high profile cases involving political figures tend to avoid true criminal prosecution because of executive privilege and preferential treatment for social hierarchy and the interpretive flexibilities of civil law. But when it comes to the confines of God's law, no one is above the law: not the Sanhedrin, not the president, not the House of Representatives, not the archbishops, not the pope no one. If His law is opposed, transgressed, or edited to accommodate insurrections, the offender is a blasphemous hypocrite and will suffer the consequences of accountability in the end. Where then should we turn for moral judgment? Certainly not to some self-absorbed political icon revered by an uninformed and misinformed populous. The purest of all is Jesus, the first and last remaining moral representative of humankind who ever lived. He tells you who He is, what and why he is going to do what he does, and He gives ample warning as to what will happen if His principles are not adhered to: "Woe be unto you lawmakers."

To clarify any misgivings about supporting Biblical documentations herein, it is not my intention to conjure categorical subtleties for mixed motives concerning which Bible is the only Bible. The basis for this work focuses more on the importance of the Word of God, not Biblical version. Also, to keep information fresh and familiar, I made a concerted effort to separate the ideas of long-held biblical proclamations from the multi-dimensional claims of rigorous complexities suggested by axiological and hermeneutical criticism. This too will simplify and centralize my arguments. Case in point, J. Dwight Pentecost says, "No question facing the student of eschatology is more important than the question of the method to be employed in the interpretation of the prophetic Scriptures."[11] Furthermore, it is my opinion that in more ways than one the implied trappings of eschatology are a major contributor to the deafening cadence of Biblical defection.

To round out the Biblical perspective on social conscience, there will be a chapter on what I prefer to call free fall to judgment. It will be at that time that my opinion on one of the most reigning questions corroborated throughout this book will be answered, and that is, without further compromising Biblical truths to accommodate man's continual fall, can Christianity as we know it survive in a society that vilifies anything that represents Christian symbolic ideology?

I

THE PARALLELS OF TRUTH AND CREATION: SHOULD THEY BE COMPROMISED?

If one should ask what the inherent truths Christians hold to be self-evident for the basis of creation are, the answer would surely include the workings of a divine God and the inalienable truths held within the book of Genesis that summarizes the creation premise. Compatible with these truths, it is my opinion that it is necessary to delineate a conceptual position for the lingering quintessential question, what is the meaning of life? This question is not subsumed by the creation premise because it is my contention that the meaning of life is linked to, and cannot be separated from, the Biblical creation story that carries with it the universal moral and ethical laws that are constant and governed by the higher power of creation. Thus, the interrelatedness of the two concepts makes it a theoretical binary principle that links the development of man's purpose and character and predetermines what kind of world we will live in. Otherwise, by what moral code could we measure the conscionable difference between good and evil? Would it be through evolutionary science, philosophy, man's law, or God's law? Think, what unprejudiced, unconditional language would present a moral code? One imperious approach is cited in Norman Geisler's book *Christian Ethics.* Geisler quotes atheist Friedrich Nietzsche as saying, "God is dead and we have killed him. When God died all objective values died with him."[1] Geisler goes on to say, "The Russian novelist Fyodor Dostoevsky noted correctly that if God is dead, then anything goes. For Nietzsche, the death of God meant not only the death of God-given values, but also the need for man to create his own values. In doing so, he argued, we must go 'beyond good and evil.' Since there is no God to will what is good, we must will our own good. And since there is no eternal value, we must will the eternal recurrence of the same state of affairs."[2] Judging from the liberal, freewill spirit of civil courts, it appears we are headed in this direction.

According to Francis Bacon, there are some serious concerns when using language. He says, "The problem is that people often use words in different ways, so words alone cannot reveal the nature of things [and] language that is not disciplined by rigorous observation of the world therefore leads to mistaken thoughts."[3] This results in a euphemism rather than actual intended meaning.

A perfect example of Bacon's viewpoint on the use of language is the word, *abomination*. Given the current state of political and newfound social sensitivities held by various groups, Scriptural clarity and specific intended use of the word tends to highly offend those who live and behave sexually contrary to the Biblical parameters governing this word. But no matter what kind of politically correct spin one uses to try to justify such behavior, scripturally and in the eyes of God this is an abomination. Deuteronomy 22:5 emphatically states, "The woman shall not wear that which pertaineth unto man, neither shall a man put on a woman's garment: for all that do so are abomination unto the Lord."[4] There are other cited poignancies, such as Romans 1:18-27 that are more explicit in spelling out the perimeter for the inerrant living guidelines in God's use of the word abomination, but there is no need to expound as the message has already been established. However, know that his warning is clear; "And mine eye shall not spare, neither will I have pity: I will recompense thee according to thy ways and thine abominations that are in the midst of thee; and ye shall know that I am the Lord that smiteth."[5]

Although the scriptural position on this matter is clear, by virtue of zealous lobbyist reformers, the word abomination has been torn from its theological base and is now perceived as irrelevant in today's liberal, redesigned, and faltering world. More troubling is the venomous guise of political correctness, which comes with the approval of morally compromised liberal courts attacking those of moral righteousness. However, an acquittal by a civil court does not necessary mean a verdict of innocence, especially when it relates to the moral conscience of the people who follow a righteous God. The truth of the matter is that when you seek the approval of purloining anti-Christian courts to force an agenda that conflicts with biblical truths it makes for a widespread, dangerous precedent. Court approval against the wishes of the moral majority maximizes commanding overall social jurisdiction that is attached only to certain lobbyist groups and not necessarily for the overall good of morally conscionable people. More importantly, bypassing the truths of Scripture to accommodate an agenda is blasphemous and similarly echoes my reigning question; can Christianity survive while compromising biblical truths to accommodate man's continual fall? Court approval of an immoral agenda should be more than enough for Christians to unite and openly ask by what fusion of conscience do lawmakers live where legalized immoral behaviors take precedence over the laws of God?

In the radical movement for transformation of society's acceptance of immorality, there is no escaping the premise that if God approved of such measures He would have made provisions for them. Those who practice or condone immoral behaviors are irritated by this premise because it exposes and denounces inappropriate human conduct. This is precisely where the doctrine of willful choice comes in. So to speak, either you believe or you don't.

Directly, the delicate balance of choice can either take you to the light of Christ or you can live in defiance and fall right in with the historical consequential sufferings of those gone before you. But because Christians are taught to turn the other cheek, this makes Christian unification against such abominations difficult. In addition, because of denominational strife, there is always the danger of one denomination absorbing the fight against these immoral intrusions, with other denominations taking advantage of this opportunity by condoning such immoral behaviors to build a larger flock and then jockeying for positions that can lead to economic and political power. Then there are Christians partaking in the very things that Christianity disavows; in a sense, creating a Christ of convenience. The saving grace in all of this is that no matter how diligently man endeavors to fade out or deaden the truths of Scripture there is no escaping that biblical truths are inextricably tied to the guiding road map for moral and ethical social continuity that beckons our undivided attention. Did he not say, "Behold, I come quickly: blessed is he that keepeth the sayings of the prophecy of this book."[6]

Indeed, God's law is set and does have preconditioned expectations that command adherence, which is why a commitment to God is difficult. But the truth of the matter is when we deviate from God's laws, Scriptural history reveals the plight of those nations who opted to abandon His law to live in sinful ways. Bacon was right when he said, "The mind has fallen into bad habits."[7]

In fairness to pedagogical diplomacy, when comparing and defending creation against evolution, the pro argument for Christian values is not to be critical of evolution without providing some long-standing and plausible evidence for creation's inherent truths. This application is paramount to the ideas proposed by this chapter, and whether this is achieved, of course, will largely depend on how well the book presents its deliberations against what biases and prejudices the reader might entertain.

Arguably, the main thrust here is not to convert but to inform. Coming to the Lord is a personal choice. But still, in comparing the two concepts, we will see that just as day and night are opposites, evolution and creation fall under the same comparative principle and are rightfully identified as mutually exclusive ideas with creation being the most logical and virtuous of the two.

To begin this comparative analysis would be to investigate in what ways the principles of God outweigh those of evolution and how evolution affects traditional creation belief. First of all, God said that "He hath made the earth by his power, he hath established the world by his wisdom, and hath stretched out the heavens by his discretion."[8] As a creature of God's creation, I have already seen that the life works of a high and most powerful God far outweigh Darwin's (1859) basic evolution model presented as, "life for all organisms as a struggle against considerable odds to survive and reproduce."[9] In the final analysis you too will see that the evolution surge is likened to those historical governments that vied to make themselves God over the doctrines of the Bible and the more recently proven-to-be-false conjured sophism that man is responsible for global warming.

In addition to its many other supporting criteria, one of the primary tenets of creationism is found in the perfection of the universe. This perfect order could not have happened without a perfect beginning, and that beginning came from creation by God, the perfect Creator. I believe science knows He is out there somewhere; otherwise the hunt to destroy Him would not be so vigilant. It's almost as though the scientific world is grieving because they were not the first to capitalize from the considerable evidence that supports the creation idea. The truth of the matter is that this issue is not to be taken lightly because the imminent danger of the evolution hypothesis does not merely begin or end with the evolution hunt per se. The ramifications of this quest run much deeper. Just as prayer was taken out of public schools in 1962, evolutionists and various arms of anti-Christian elements are diligently working to "legitimize and legalize" the evolution theory in the very same public schools where prayer had been outlawed. This event is not a simple matter of separation of church and state. It is a willful and direct attack on Christianity and another means by which the anti-Christian movement can consternate Christian ideology. In a literal sense, for science and government to methodically eradicate God as the foundation of life, what can be said about our leadership's adherence to the guiding truths of our nation's constitution? In other words, yes, there might be a God, but so what?

Unable to free themselves from such an entrenched position, those in opposition to Christianity tend to forget that God's existence and commanding Word are not to be mocked or taken lightly, for He warns of retaliatory measures. This vengeance is clearly spelled out in John 3:36: "He that believeth on the Son hath everlasting life: and he that believeth not the Son shall not see life; but the wrath of God abideth on him."[10] Despite countless evidence of God's existing power, misbelieving evolutionists and their followers still fail to acknowledge the obvious gifts and vengeances from a creation God.

Irrespective of the customary, unwholesome scientific determinants concerning the creation story, what tends to be slighted and minimized is the fact that past history of the beginning self is not predicated on scientific facts and theories. Origin of self comes from a law that offers by choice, salvation or damnation. Deviation from this law determines the type of life one will live now and for eternity not by laboratory determinates. The power of the law allows anyone to avoid the grasp of evil if only they would willfully live by the law. Given the absolutism of this law, how they are going to disprove a creation God now that they are responsible for igniting the question is problematic for science. On the other hand, Christianity does not have to prove God's existence. Belief in the creation God started long before science and continues to be in motion not only in a historical sense but also in the fulfillment of prophecy. This is what makes the creation and evolution controversy so interesting. Page by page prophecy unfolds, and the double edge sword provoked by evolutionists and those trying to prove that a man-like God never existed continues to stymie this virulent pretext.

When we examine the intrinsic argument for evolution's hunt, it goes something like this. It is not possible that anything so complex and breathtaking could be created without leaving an all-encompassing and definitive trace of the methodological system inherent to its origins assigned and proclaimed by a creative God. Aside from the many unanswered questions, in the hunt to disprove a creation God, the mantra of science maintains the belief that there has to be a way to measure God. My question is, why bother to measure the footsteps of Jesus when His truths were taught openly? He not only used parables to teach his message, but it would be prudent to search for yourself and see that He often incorporated His warnings in His teachings. These warnings are evidenced in Luke 21: 29-36.

As if science doesn't have enough to contend with, strengthening the argument for the physical Biblical creation story is not limited to the written form of Scripture. If we look to the invigorating arena of archeological discoveries, we see that with each new find comes supporting evidence for a biblical site that coincides with its historical place as told in Scripture. According to this model, the historical application of Biblical stories goes from words to actuaries. Although not necessary, from this position we can then postulate that eventually man's archeological discoveries will indisputably prove once and for all the creation story justifying the Christian theological precepts held in the one God housed in the Father, the Son, and the Holy Spirit. More importantly, new archeological discoveries will help to eradicate all traces of suggestiveness that Christians blindly

follow a God simply by the theological principles of faith. It will be at this
point in time that the final chapter will be written, bringing to a close the
argument between creation and the evolution proclamations held by the
fruitless whims of scientific pursuit.

When witnessing for the strengths of creation, we see that the
creation model has exhibited the ability to withstand some of the deepest
denigration from critical analysis. This is largely due to the primary
position of applied science comparing its concocted laboratory hypotheses
against the stewardship of faith, the most powerful working basic element
of Christian doctrine. Exemplary to that effect is Kierkegaard's view of the
"Wholly other." Kierkegaard says,

> Human reason can neither prove Him nor know Him.
> God is beyond the reach of reason altogether. God is the
> unknown something with which the reason collide when
> inspired by its paradoxical passion, with the result of
> unsettling even man's knowledge of himself. For whose
> sake is it that the proof is sought? Faith does not need it;
> aye, it must even regard proof as an enemy. It is only when
> faith thus begins to lose its passion, when faith begins to
> cease to be faith, that a proof becomes necessary so as to
> command respect from the side of unbelief. If God does
> not exist it would of course impossible to prove it; and if
> he does exist it would be folly to attempt it.[11]

As the creation model remains steadfast in its proclamations, it is
not surprising that the evolution model arduously fumbles with trying to
close the door on what lies beyond their agreement on at least the known
constants of the universe.

Adding to the scientific quagmire, what makes the evolution journey
so cumbersome is that it is difficult to oppose another hypothesis when
thinking is at a completely different level of inquiry and acceptance,
especially when the criteria are based on an intentional iconoclastic
position. From such a compromised base, the end result could only be
vague supporting propositions generated from established, speculative,
theoretical scientific principles rooted in the sole aim to reconstruct
rather than prove the origin of man. This is not only an insult to the
hallmarks of Christian doctrine, but this type of defamation contributes
to the immoral and unethical social conscience that Christianity does
not support. Rewriting and repressing the good news of Jesus' message
can only mean one of two things. Either the left arm of science has an
unannounced political agenda that exceeds wholesome scientific inquiry,
or Satan literally has his hand in the mix. Until this question is answered,

we won't really know. But what we do know for certain is how dictatorial governments rule when there is an absence of God.

From my point of view there will never be enough scientific evidence to preclude the universal evidences for the existence of a creation God because just by virtue of everyday life's fundamental presentations, the divine God is everywhere. The constants of God and His true science are evidenced all around us, working efficiently and effectively just as He planned. The sun comes up, and the sun goes down. The tide comes in, and the tide goes out. Seasons are sequential; what goes up must come down; and above all, there is a time to live and a time to die. What I find more astounding is that the earth spins tied to its axis and nowhere to be found is one sliver of man-made duct tape. To their own amazement, the more science digs, the more it discovers that the truths of today are the very same truths held by and from the created but perilous beginning.

Although there are evidences for hard science deductions concerning the natural constants of the universe, the link to all of these theoretical precepts should not be construed merely as a precursor to that yet to be found "something." That something they seek but cannot measure is the power of God housed in His Son, the Lord Jesus Christ. Subsequently, science must learn to accept that Christ cannot be found in a diagnostic measurement. He is the Son of God expressed in a divine principle fundamentally enforced by the unwavering principle of faith. To know Him is to believe in Him, and to believe in Him, the implied principle of faith allows you to know Him. The power of faith is especially evidenced in the forthcoming tribulation, which is supported in Hebrews 11:1-40 and by Dwight Pentecost who says "salvation in the tribulation will certainly be on the faith principle."[12]

To the benefit of the creation model, a major contribution from the evolution hypothesis is that science declares a specific level of intelligence in certain apes, which suggests there is a missing link in the evolutionary process that separates apes from man. Logically, whether due to low self-esteem or psychological duress, to say man comes from apes is juvenile. Not only that, in preservation for the dignity of man, it would be seemingly fit to portray man as a creation by God rather than a descendant of apes. To speculate that we are descendants of apes is blasphemous and quite frankly, self-incriminating for those who believe such nonsense. In fact, I think it is rather humorous that the brighter minds of mankind are looking to the DNA of monkeys and apes with hopes of understanding the psychologies of what makes man tick. Furthermore, given that science has determined that the extinction of the Neanderthal man occurred largely because of the inability to adapt to change, then would this mean that Darwin's natural selection is responsible for bringing us to the state we are? I emphatically say no even to neo-Darwinism and its implication of natural selection because what the extinction of the Neanderthal man does is further support the Biblical claim that man as we know him did not become man until God breathed the Holy Spirit and the breath of life to make him human. "And the Lord God formed man of the dust of the ground, and breathed into his nostrils the breath of life, and man became a living soul."[13]

Withdrawing from even the slightest treatment of speculative science, the breath of life separates us more than ever from scientific conclusions concerning the discovery and determinations in reference to ancient bones resembling man. Mistrusting these convenient conclusions, I implore you that we would have to consider by what process science concludes the bones to be millions of years old. Just because diagnostic instruments measure something does not necessarily mean the measurement is true. More importantly, science would have to prove that these "million-year-old people" had a soul and spirit; otherwise man as we know him is approximately six thousand years old, just as the pearls of Genesis teach.

Scientific explanations for the geological age of earth have their place as well as the discovery of ancient bones, but it is Scripture's acknowledging the breath of life that keeps solid the argument for the age of man. Furthermore, no matter what differences of opinion still exist between evolution and creation, what destroys the evolution model is that in every aspect of created creatures and plants, merely by God's ordained biological principles there is some form of God-given adaptability that keeps them from becoming extinct not evolutionary determinates.

Extending beyond its nonsensical theme for the origin of man, one of science's most constructive contributions is that we can now hypothesize and theoretically measure the mass volume of negative worldly indulgences simply by weighing the consequential suffering of social ills generated by choices away from God. Specifically, lawlessness in and out of the home denigrates self-worth, which translates to risk-taking behaviors that ultimately show up in maladaptive assaults against every aspect of moral social regulation. This happens largely because we have taken the essence of God out of public prominence and parents have failed to introduce their children to the teachings of God. Instead, we see that "God is substituted for indulgences making the popular flexible term 'way of life' vague if only because it represents not only explicit ideals of conduct deliberately chosen, but also ideals which have not been made explicit, or formulated, and which may be expressions of not only full conscious preferences, feelings, and ambitions."[14] Judging from the prominence of social immorality and its resulting influences on societal disintegration, it is obvious that these are not the doings of a righteous creation God. They derive from free will, as does the inefficacious zeal of evolutionary thinking.

I tend to view the previous paragraph as an integrated extension of how and why Scripture is clear about its expectations, preferences, and formulations as to how and why we should use Christ as the model for living. Christians do fail, but focusing on Christ is what keeps Christians from failing completely. Commitment, of course, is difficult because the short-term effects of personal desires and wants outside the domain of Christ are far more enticing than a long-term promise, which disallows drifting from the center. The problem with short-term thinking is that there is a tendency to become complacent about living in self-induced conflict. In effect, this type of living becomes the worst enemy for pursuing and experiencing goodness. Rather than more money and instant gratification, a change of heart is needed.

Support for the aforementioned words is found in the book *Mere Morality-What God Expects from Ordinary People* by Lewis B. Smeade. Smeade quotes Kierkegaard as saying; "We spend our lives building mansions for ourselves but choose to live in a dog house."[15] This observation is critical because the classic Christian model for life is that we don't just live a certain way and then die. There are guidelines, principles, codes for morality, and ethics all intertwined with one God housed in and reborn by the physical arrival of Christ on earth. His primary mission was to teach us salvation on the road to His grace, thereby destroying the evil works of Satan. We gain His grace by choices we make, and those choices are governed by abstinence from those behaviors contrary to the essential elements of God's primary law that is intended to keep us forever in His kingdom; least we should never forget there is a judgment day. Satan is alive and well.

For the unbeliever, if a creation God does not seem plausible, then from what guiding source will the deterrents from evil derive? To what end is there meaning to life? Some might say from the controlling conscience within, and others might say from the radical changes and adaptation to an environment governed by abhorrence. Wholeheartedly, I say if Christ the God is not the Creator and Redeemer, then the only alternative in the universe is the risky and doubtful hypothesis of evolution, which has to quantify theoretical scientific proof how morals and contractual agreement came from apes.

Ironically, calculating the avenues for criticism of Biblical truths is not limited to opposing viewpoints between science and creationists. A great deal also comes from various departees from mainstream Christian theological groups who profess their own interpretation of Scripture to be no less than pearls of wisdom for all ages. Then there is the overabundance of new schools of thought, and the staple bin of philosophers and theologians who present newfound summations as gospel. 2Timothy 4:3–4 warns of these postulates. "For the time will come when they will not endure sound doctrine; but after their own lusts shall they heap to themselves teachers, having itching ears; and they shall turn away their ears from the truth, and shall be turned into fables"[16] Thus, in my understanding of Scripture neither man nor priest can give or teach truths if they do not come from the Holy Spirit housed in the Book itself.

In reference to the previous paragraph, one of the most noteworthy examples of turning a deaf ear to truth is centered on the parallel between how the priestly Sanhedrin used false accusations to eradicate Christ and his message. Another example can be found in what ultramodern evolutionists and various anti-Christian organizations are doing to destroy the same truths. One such group that is discussed later in the book is the Jesus Seminar. The sole purpose for this group is to destroy the image of Jesus and to go as far as to say that there never was a man called Jesus Christ. I submit to you from what kind of conscience do such thoughts derive; more importantly, to what avail?

In reply to this question I have to say by pulling the trigger on their own demise it may be too late for ant-Christian sentiment to see that it will take more than the words of men to dethrone the established Word of God. You might ask, I thought it was never too late to repent! Of course it's never too late, but one has to have a genuinely repenting heart before he can make the change. Adamancy that there is no God disqualifies those, without the help of God, from reaching a repenting position. This surely indicates that some will be saved to eternal life and others will flounder in the tormenting "mental pits" of Hades. "Watch ye therefore, and pray always, that ye may be accounted worthy to escape all these things that shall come to pass, and to stand before the Son of man."[17]

It's not enough that Scripture has all the external strife of hermeneutical and axiological debate on the exactitudes of intent and meaning, let alone having to contend with the peripheral anti-Christian groups, such as the Jesus Seminar. Although these variants have yet to succeed in their goal of dismembering Christian ideology, they remain a menacing aberrated force to reckon with.

In terms of professing and relying on the strength of Scripture and the Lord, the one question that always seems to dominate the pool of inquiry is what makes one think that Jesus is the answer and only way to heaven? The answer to this question is relatively simple and is found in the intrinsic structural content of Scripture. In John 14:6 Jesus says, "I am the way, the truth, and the life: no man cometh to the Father, but by me."[18] But the resonating force of this proclamation, of course, can only work to your benefit if you have faith in Christ. More astounding, if you do have faith in Christ and do not tempt the Lord, He is emphatic about rewarding your faith. "If ye shall ask anything in my name, I will do it" (John 14:14).[19] This is not a limited warranty, it's an eternal guarantee.

More than anything, the one principle that truly separates creation and evolution is that the one bases itself on invective scientific principles and the other is predicated on a relentless reciprocal faith in a God who promises and delivers exactly what He promises if man would only live by His law. This is not to say that science is completely ostracized from playing a role in God's work. In Edward F. Hill's book *The King James Version Defended: A Christian View of the New Testament Manuscripts*, Hill says, "The guidance of the Bible is necessary in the study of natural sciences. In the Bible God has inscribed the basic principles which give unity to scientific thought and provide the answers to ultimate scientific questions."[20] But the scientific aspect of what Hill speaks is of a different nature; the one held in terms of "God's works of creation and providence"[21] and not the one that diligently works trying to disprove His existence.

Tied to creation is one of the most indicative prerequisites for living a Godly life: making a sincere effort to forgo those behaviors that are commonly known as sin. How this relates to creation is spelled out in a basic formula. Before the fall, man was perfect in every respect. After the fall, the creation story unfolded with perfection succumbing to conscionable reason, and reason giving way to choices, and choices giving way to suffering, and suffering giving way to justification and projection of blame for sin, and then chastisement of God for allowing all these horrible things to continue. All this and more visibly related to the life-giving dance exemplified through the inner God of fallen man. The truth of the matter is "Why blame God for what man has brought upon himself? Man has been dancing to the music of a godless civilization; it has been a war dance in worship of force. Now that he has to pay the fiddler, why blame God? He has withdrawn [His] restraints, and what is man experiencing? This is merely the operation of the law of sowing and reaping!"[22] This is exactly why organized religion should never lose sight of practicing and teaching the Christian trademarks of morality and ethics. Otherwise, where will mankind be?

Where creation sometimes gets itself into eschatological debate is when theological "hunters" profess that because the creation story comes from oral traditions and was then later written, isn't it likely that the written version does not truly represent the oral because somewhere down the line through its original and many translations Scripture should concede to the possibility of dramatic error? Not to avoid the question, but to simply call these writings man-made stories or exaggerated fabrications wouldn't say too much for any of man's past, current, or future postulations on life. The creation story and all the writings thereafter are proven prophecies to have come from the Light and were given by inspiration to select authors so that the words of Romans 8:28 and the likes will resonate for all time. "And we know that all things work together for good to them that love God, to them who are called according to his purpose."[23]

In support of the previous statement is Norman L. Geisler. Geisler says, "The writings are authoritative, not because of the human author, but because God is regarded as the ultimate author. The human authors are real authors; there is no idea of mechanical dictation. Nonetheless, God's Spirit spoke through them, and it is the divine authorship that gives their writing unique importance."[24] Thus, the combination of writings and an unwavering faith are the backbone of creation, with creation displaying the final result of God's work manifested through a glorious reality.

Evolution cannot win the battle of the minds simply by referring to the proven oracles of Scripture as mistranslated and misprinted fiction. They will have to produce conclusive evidence to support their argument if they want to knock creation off its hallowed pedestal. Because evolution has yet to provide such definitive data, it is safe to say that the creation argument emphatically rules as evolution continues to lie in a hypothesis built on an alluvium displayed in a composite of inconclusive facts and figures. Just by virtue of man's aberrant ways is enough to prove there is a God who expects more from His creation. Left to himself, man would surely self-destruct. I would venture to say that Darwin himself considered his ideas to be mistakenly radical, but the one place he might be accurate is in his hypothesis is that we all struggle for survival. These jeweled ideas come directly from Genesis 3:19: "In the sweat of thy face shalt thou eat bread, till thou return unto the ground."[24]

Is it a sin to willfully discredit the creation God? First of all, the answer to this question has two parts. For one, those who study and believe Scripture and try to live up to the laws of God know that original sin is not something simply fabricated by man-made religious doctrine simply to hold people hostage by guilt. If you are a conscionable God-fearing person, guilt is a natural response to sinning because awareness of sin encompasses the behavior or thinking that is contrary to God's law. Any thinking and behavior contrary to that law is thus labeled as sin. This is not to say that all people are conscious of sin because many do unconscionable things under the antisocial premise of, "I'll get you before you get me" without experiencing a smidgen of guilt. In fact, who can forget that the Sanhedrin led very sinful lives but never experienced such heavy guilt or animosity until Jesus publicly exposed them by pointing out their hypocrisy? As a result, their hate shifted from hating the Romans to finding ways to destroy Jesus. Essentially, they were likened to high-profile attorneys charged with upholding the law but using the law to get around the law. Simply put, sin is a word that encompasses all those ideas, concepts, and behaviors that are contrary to God's law originally induced into man by the original sin of Adam and Eve. No truer meaning of sin is that which is expressed by

Arthur Pink. "To Adam and Eve, God preached the blessed and basic truth of substitution- the just dying for the unjust, the innocent suffering for the guilty. Adam and Eve were guilty and merited destruction, but these animals died in their stead, and by their death a covering was provided to hide their sin and shame."[25]

Although admirable, to become richly consistent in God's way is not easily achieved because essentially, from the choice made by our original parents, we are born into sin. Given this presupposition, not adhering to the laws of the creation God is bad enough, but when you know the difference and continue to sin, this is more detrimental in the eyes of God. Specifically, despite His gift of repentance, there comes a time when personal accountability and responsibility have to play some role in a man's integrity and character, otherwise he could easily be labeled as a product of the evolution model without having to produce an explanation for the soul and spirit.

Outside the constraints of the aforementioned model, the journey for the nonbelievers and the evolutionists is much simpler because its proponents and followers are adamant about not believing there is a creation God; therefore, they don't have to abide by His principals or be held accountable. But in so many ways, climbing this mountain without God is proving itself to be a monumental and fruitless task for evolutionists, not to mention its negative contributions to the discombobulated society we see. This is exactly why I believe that the antichrist is more than an actual specific person as Revelation ascribes. I believe it is an embodied movement that circulates throughout every aspect of man's subjective and objective conscience, and any leader or group who denounces Christ contributes to the whole idea of the antichrist. The Sanhedrin is alive and well.

As pointed out earlier, avoiding sin is an ongoing battle for anyone, and attesting to this fact we see one of the most saintly and trusted apostles of Christ who had great difficulty meeting this obligation. In Romans 7:14-15 Paul confesses, "For we know that the law is spiritual: but I am carnal, sold under sin. For that which I do I allow not: for what I would, that do I not; but what I hate, that do I."[27] The task tied to the strength of this particular passage is a repented heart-not only after knowingly committing a sin, but after committing a sin and not repeating the same mistake. This is where and when genuine salvation and grace come together.

Irrefutably, no matter how much man tries to escape or defer the clutches of God's law, there is no escaping this ultra constant law because His watchful presence is forever working in the wages against sin in most anything and everything that transpires during the course of a day. To the benefit of mankind, the inerrancy of God's law does not only apply to a select few. By believing, watching, and listening, the Holy Spirit will guide anyone in all that they do if only they would ask. These contingencies are an important application because without them, benefits in the hunt for abstention cannot otherwise be achieved.

Francis A. Schaeffer defines the impact and significance of God's law in his work *A Christian Manifesto*. He says, "All men, even the king, are under the law and not above it."[28] The implication is that even government is under God's law; although government would like to believe they are God's law. Evolution then cannot refute Schaeffer's statement because evolution has little to do with the development of intrinsic conscionable moral and ethical law, the intellect, or the volatile behavioral psychological profile for character endowed with spirit and soul. The constructs for these attributes run much deeper and essentially are derived from a creation God and are influenced by what I choose to call a two-fold theoretical model.

First, in his text *Assessment of Children*, Jerome M. Sattler states that the features of character and personality are a "direct result of genetic and environmental factors."[29] This premise is nothing new, as it is the footstool for behavioral psychology. Second, from a Christian perspective, it is the belief that God created man in His own likeness and endowed each of us with the created physical and mental mechanics for ethical, moral, and intellectual development. Out of these working virtues come "the conflicts between different values-justice and kindness, loyalty and fairness, honesty and the will to please [all] paralleled, inevitably, by conflicts between prohibitions.[30] Irrefutably, it all goes back to having to make the choice between good and evil, which evolution cannot explain.

Notably, despite all the strides science has contributed to making the world a better place, technical information relative to the biological evolution argument can only go so far, making this issue not only unsolvable but also easily defeated. I say this because despite severe critical analysis since its conception, the phenomena of Scripture maintain the privilege of standing alone in history unparalleled by any other document or scientific model. Geisler adds to this contention when he says, "Scientific progress' is an ambiguous term used to justify almost anything else we desire to do. This argument absolutizes scientific progress as the norm by which all else is justified ... science deals with what is, not with what ought to be."[31] What ought to be comes from the applied moral principles of God. As stated earlier, Geisler contends, "Since God made the rules, it is simply our duty to keep them and leave the results in His hands."[32]

Essentially, for all intents and practical purposes, the creation argument has been settled by the philosophical construct that we cannot deny what truly is, which is that the reality of God's laws and consequences govern the creation model and all its precepts by a higher creation God. In the final analysis, all inquiry points to the fact that, "there is no real evidence that the present race was produced by any naturalistic evolutionary process. Both Scripture and the scientific evidence point to God as the cause of the human species."[33] This proclamation is supported by the fact that, "science with all its technology and touted brilliance has not been able to permanently improve even a fruit fly."[34] God lets science tinker, but He is not naïve or foolish enough to let His finely tuned secrets be known to man who has desecrated and intentionally ignored every law that is intended for salvation on the way to grace. Because man cannot remain true to these laws, I would hate to think what man would do with the power of God if he discovered the untouchable and hidden precepts of God. This is a frightening thought because 1Samuel 24:13 warns: "As saith the proverb of the ancients, Wickedness proceedeth from the wicked: but mine hand shall not be upon thee." [34]

Among the many unanswered questions tied to the evolution model, two of the most visible that it has been unable to answer are where did the conscience derive from and when is the starting point for conscience? Donald M. Broom seems to have similar concerns. He says, "There is a widespread view in many human societies that we are all endowed with a conscience. The conscience, which is thought to lead to feelings such as remorse, guilt and shame, should block some anti-social behavior and promote good actions … the key questions concern where the conscience comes from and how it acts."[36] This interpretation adds to my own argument, but the next question is at what point in the evolutionary process did man use that conscience to determine the difference between good and evil? And if man is indeed a by-product of evolutionary steps, shouldn't it be that each man would be an exact replication in every aspect of the evolution process? As far as the eye can see there is no evidence of this in any of my fellow man. Should science prove that physical and biological evolution is the beginning of man, this is still only one piece of the puzzle.

Much to science's chagrin, it cannot close the door on creation because it will also need to prove from where and how two of the most contingent sovereign components of man, spirit, and soul manifest themselves if they did not come from a creation God. This is exactly why I do not believe that evolutionary false-work will ever stand firmly by itself. To the contrary, Genesis 2:7 tells us exactly from where these components derive and that is: "God breathed life into man and man became a living soul."[36] These words hold a sacred place in the creation oracles, and the likelihood of an unbelieving evolutionist ever discovering the intrinsic secret to their manifestation is most definitely safeguarded from sedition.

Again, from the creationist perspective, the book of Genesis tells us about a human made in God's image having a soul and spirit, but more than the actual Biblical writings themselves, these two passages are the power, ordonnance, and purpose for the complete story and wholeness of man's beginning. These holy substances are the unattainable "something" unaccounted for in the evolution theoretical model. Even as such, what we do know for sure is the more man moves away from the defining central truths of Scripture and its prescriptions for morality and ethics, we see a higher level of unconscionable trouble generating deficits in the behaviors of man. This is nothing new. Long before guns were invented, man had a natural proclivity for killing, be it rock, knife, sword, ball and chain, or long bow. Ironically, the modern-day liberals want to ban all guns, and religion is blamed for all wars. According to my opinion on such matters, man is endowed with all sorts of weapons, which in most cases are exhibited through psychological torment that surfaces as social warfare derived from the beholder's mind. Some call it the sign of the times, others say it is economically driven, others call it the new frontier of man's evolution, and some gladly confess that maybe it is the decline of "old" traditional religious dogma. I am more inclined to believe much of societal declination is due to a lack of moral discernment generated by anti-God sentiment and teaching supported by a socialist governing mentality absent of God.

The implication here is not to say that you cannot have a good life unless you are a Christian who believes in the creation model. Non-Christians and even atheists portray a conscionable life. But in order to remain grounded in some resemblance of morality we have to ask the question: What implied structure or meaning to life would be based on an evolution model? Because these articles have yet to be announced, this is one good reason why the central components of religion have greater value. Geisler says, "Hence the tests of truth involve logical noncontradiction, empirical fit, and existential viability. In affirming that the human words of the Bible are inerrant or true, I am saying that their teaching is noncontradictory, factual, and visible. One who stakes his life on their teaching will not be disappointed."[38] Lest we never forget that the teacher teaches, but the burden of proof falls upon the student.

Throughout this chapter I have introduced and touched on a broad range of topics and questions, several of which I am sure have room for greater survey. The one in particular that I find the most poignant is the argument from evolution science. It is not that Christianity hasn't been attacked before, but evolution has gone further than any other adversary by willfully denying the very fact that there is a creation God. For two reasons I find this to be troubling. First, it is a direct attack on Christianity but by the standards held by political correctness, coming to Christian defense does not meet the guidelines for protection by the liberal courts. Two, the motivation to disprove the existence of a divine God and what will be done with the information has yet to be announced by the scientific community. This in itself is both puzzling and frightening because any time science seeks to make things better, generally a spokesperson publicly reveals motivation, intent, and findings. Merely attesting that there is "something" out there does not qualify as a respectful recognition for a divine God. Nor does it reveal the motivation as to why science is so preoccupied with disproving the Christian God that exists in the one God housed in the Trinity of the Father, The Son, and the Holy Spirit. Why this question needs to be answered is self-evident in man's continued inability to control self-indulgences that are detrimental to the well-being of the world community. As Christians, not only do we need to protect the oracles of God, we need to act accordingly to the guidelines of Scripture so as to determine what kind of life the next generation will live. Somehow I get the notion that the goal is not to disprove the creation story as much as it is to completely eliminate the ideals of Christian doctrine for a greater political purpose.

No doubt my position on the subject of evolution versus creation is rather critical. I choose to be critical because my Christian conscience sees the sheer recklessness of godless scientific proclamations erroneously weighted against the inerrant truths held by Scripture. Evolution keeps moving forward by commercial packaging in much the same way as man is blamed for global warning or a president who only after six months in office receives a Nobel Peace Prize which he himself is quoted as saying that he isn't sure he's done enough to earn it. This type of manipulative propaganda even exceeds the sewer pipe absurdities demonstrated by idolized and self-aggrandized showbiz personalities. As a believer, I cannot help but view the scientific effort more as an antagonist and perpetrator than a direct contributor that replicates the common good of the Christian view for moral and ethical preservation.

Compared to Scripture's six thousand year history, science is youthful. To put God on trial through scientific edifications underscores why there needs to be a consorted Christian effort to safeguard against counterfactual sentiments from so many blasphemous opposing forces. Aside from the fact that these threats are real, I feel comfortable in knowing that the power and foundation of creation is not predicated on an unwonted God. He is and always will be in charge, and He does get angry.

God's wrath is not a hapless coincidence. It is always provoked. Biblical history shows when necessary he reproofs all that oppose or defy His expectations. His wrath is felt in earthquakes, floods, famine, drought, monumental fires, wars, and rumors of war. In fact, these disasters are plentiful with more to come. Provoking such disasters is the U.S. president's comment: "We are no longer a Christian nation." Before and since that time, the United States has seen floods, drought, dust storms, tornados, and fires in unprecedented numbers, severe major economic downturn, new wars, and rumors of war all in Biblical proportion, as well as a 5.9 earthquake in Washington, D.C., in August of 2011. From January to the beginning of March 2012, on record are over 125 tornadoes, some of which have caused loss of life and damage, and the tornado season has yet to begin. The biggest tornado, however, will be experienced in the forthcoming inevitable world war between radical Islam, Christianity, and all those nations against Israel. As stated earlier, these signs are not mere coincidences. "And your strength shall be spent in vain: for your land shall not yield her increase, neither shall the trees of the land yield their fruits."[39] America is paying a price for turning its back on God, but more dangerous is America's determination to bargain away God's city of Jerusalem. God clearly warns, "And unto his son will I give one tribe, that David my servant may have a light always before me in Jerusalem, the city which I have chosen me to put my name there."[40] In preservation of our country, it is wise to never forget that, "When the Jews re-formed Israel in 1948, reunited Jerusalem as the capital in 1967, and annexed their original Promised Land with the 1948 Israeli boundaries, God restored His promise to Abraham and David. [So] when a world leader demands a division of the land, he or she is actually coming against the covenant that God created with His own name."[41] Just to acquire the praise of men or to put your name on record as the mediator for creating a Palestinian State at the expense of the Jews is not prudent. The sins of such parents will surely fall upon the heads of their children. America and the world must never forget that "the Jewish people existed and exists, according to the Scripture, as ever-present evidence that the plan and purpose were of God."[42]

Once proud, moving from God has transformed America's people into a maladaptive population basking in a sense of entitlement exempt from personal responsibility and accountability and collectively unionizing for all the wrong reasons. This newfound mental and behavioral revolution has made America an immoral and unconscionable nation, putting "In God We Trust" in jeopardy while at the same time causing a government-reliant populous waiting for a handout. If God's believers allow this social insurrection to continue, we will lose our autonomy and ability to choose what kind of people we would want to crowd us out in line at the grocery store. Like it or not, it is the ingenuity of the Jews and Christians that work to safeguard the cornerstones of common decency and human dignity, not those in charge of government.

Whether or not this chapter has satisfied your appetite for conclusive evidence for a creation God, the intent was to show how the creation story is the connecting link for man's relationship with God. The question is if Christianity fails, from what well of wisdom would we draw upon to measure ethics and morals for preservation of God's ultimate destiny for man? What will happen to the hallmarks of goodness that have made America great, and how far will the newfound way of life go to satisfy its reckless appetite for the heresy of political "change"?

In conclusion, for those individuals who find it necessary to tie the sanctity of Christian principles to the bloodshed of the Crusades, as I stated earlier, I openly confess that mainstream denominational Christians have also fallen from grace. But for now, Biblical facts and reasonable conclusions drawn from those facts have proven themselves to be in the best interest and method for the survival of mankind, and by His authority and His authority alone, evolution theoretical models will remain just that. "Though I bear record of myself, yet my record is true: for I know whence I came, and whether I go; but ye cannot tell whence I come, and whether I go."[43]

II

EASTERN ORTHODOXY AND ITS PERSECUTIONS

Leaving behind the brief summary on social degradation, anti-Christian movements, and glaring theoretical differences between creation and evolution, this would be a good time to interject some thoughts on the early persecutions of the Christian Church; in particular those of the Eastern Orthodox Church. After all, persecution of the Christian Church and its doctrines is the emphasis of this book. Foremost, we must understand that, within the realm of Christian persecutions, today's Christian bloodshed is not any different from those sufferings of yesteryear. Shamefully, the world's laissez-faire response also has not changed. The International Tribunal sits in high-backed chairs as churches are burned and Christians are beheaded, and the UN invisibly stands by as a buffer zone while Somalia boasts, "There are no Christians in Somalia. We killed them all." Reportedly, the last known Christian bishop in Somalia was killed in 2011. "In such nations as the Sudan and parts of Nigeria today, armed Muslim warriors enter villages demanding the entire village to meet together. Those who convert to Islam are spared. Those who do not are killed to create fear. Often, the men are killed while the wives and daughters are raped and the children taken and raised as Muslims."[1] The frightening thought is we do not have to go to the Middle East, China, Russia, or Africa to witness Christian persecutions. To a large degree, persecutions are happening right here in America, but, at this point in time, only recognizable through the legal system.

This particular chapter is intended to show the severity of such inhumane practices that exist even within the ranks of Christianity. Its contents are a researched presentation of historical facts about the atrocities that culminated because of doctrinal differences between Eastern Orthodoxy and Western Roman Catholicism during the quest for controlling denominational power. Strangely, much of the forthcoming data is not known to the ordinary citizen. In fact, other than Orthodox practitioners, very few know that a large segment of Eastern Orthodoxy celebrates Christmas on January 7 and New Year's on January 14, which is according to the Julian calendar. Pointedly, the religious strife suffered by Eastern Orthodoxy is not only pertinent to Christianity. There are deep divisions in Islam, as seen by the doctrinal strains between the Sunni and Shiite Muslims.

No doubt, Christianity with its many divisions and offshoot churches has been its own worst enemy, which is why we should never forget the wisdom of Paul in 1 Corinthians 12:13: "For by one Spirit are we all baptized into one body whether we be Jews or Gentiles, whether we be bond or free; and have been all made to drink into one Spirit."[2] Therefore, to fully appreciate the propositional ambitions and attitudes of this chapter, I suggest you leave all your denominational prejudices behind and embrace the most fundamental element of Jesus' teachings: to love one another as He loved us.

I chose to discuss the Eastern Orthodox religion because despite its many persecutions, Orthodoxy has managed to carry on with its rich apostolic traditions derived from the earliest churches of Judea and Thessalonica. There is something to be said for such a faithful and tenacious character.

By last estimates, there are approximately 300 million Eastern Orthodox Christians worldwide. History shows that much of its development, preservation, and autonomy have been heavily entrenched in insurmountable attacks and oppression from cultural differences stemming from Muslim domination to the political and religious problems of the Western half of the Roman Empire. In fact, the problems that came with the AD 1054 division of the Roman Empire have never been reconciled to this day. AD 1054, however, should not be construed as the ultimate beginning of the great schism. "The schism was something that came about gradually through a long and complicated process, starting well before the eleventh century and not completed until sometime later."[3] No doubt the book of Acts remains the cornerstone of Christian Church history, but even as such, the political and religious differences between the Eastern and Western Roman Empire could not curtail the eventual split of the Catholic Church.

Long before Roman persecution and control, early church belief and organization was predicated on an organized society without any kind of major opposition between spirit and form or between freedom and organization. Meeting in homes, caves, stables, or barns, it was a united church centered on Jesus Christ, free from bias or prejudice. This is evidenced when Paul called the church the body of Christ and the life of grace in 1 Corinthians 12:13: "and have been all made to drink into one Spirit."[4]

Over time, the spirit of the church moved from meeting in caves and homes into designated buildings with an organized hierarchical structure and a doctrine that would identify a particular Christian group. Out of this process evolved the Eastern and Western Catholics. Although a comparative analysis of the two Catholic churches reveals many doctrinal differences, where Eastern and Westerns Catholics still greatly differ is that the Eastern Orthodox Church has endeavored to maintain the earliest doctrines of Christian formal church organization derived from the Apostolic Church and the Nicene Council determinates. This is especially evidenced in the application of the liturgy, the Eucharist, and the interpretation and role of Christ and the Virgin Mary. Committed to the significance of that faith, the Orthodox Church remains true to form but isolated. If all of Christianity would come together, they would know that Jesus Christ is the same person for all denominations and died as such. "Therefore let all the house of Israel know assuredly, that God hath made that same Jesus Christ, whom ye have crucified, both Lord and Christ."[5]

Defending apostolic doctrine was an ongoing process for the original apostles, and this tradition still carries on today through the Orthodox Church. As Jesus' church continued to grow, it was obvious that something had to be done to curtail all the internal bickering that was clearly exemplified by the Western and Eastern churches. What better time for each group to express and defend themselves than when the Roman Empire was split into two major geographical sectors. Each sector had its own Emperor-Constantine to the East and Maxentius to the West. No doubt the Western Roman Empire felt it benefited from the split, but this geographical split actually lent itself to being the beginning of the Eastern Orthodox religion by announcing the contents of its own identity. This identity derives from the original apostolic church as defined by the standards of Judea, Thessalonica, and the Nicene Councils, but not by the determinants of Rome.

When it comes to personal contributions, no one individual contributed more to the spirit and salvation of Eastern Orthodoxy than Emperor Constantine. Although he was not a Christian, during his reign, Eastern Orthodoxy became the official church of the Byzantine Empire. Since that time, even with the destruction of the Byzantine Empire by the Turks, the Eastern church has maintained a full stream of New Testament faith, worship, and religious practice, all while enduring great persecution.

Despite the growth of Rome's acceptance of Christianity, there were still a variety of exotic cults that were running rampant throughout the empire. Some of the cultic gods served as symbols of national-political religion. This national-political religion was neither a system of beliefs nor a system of morals. It was a ritual of sacrifices and prayers that resembled more of a cult that satisfied a primary political and state significance. As an expression of loyalty, all that was required for Roman citizens was to display outward participation in the state cult. To do so, the only thing they had to do was to "burn a few sticks of incense before the images of the national gods, call the emperor "lord," and celebrate the rites."[6]

As Christianity started to grow, the Romans did not perceive the Christians as much of a threat at first. They equated them to the Jews who already had an accepted and established religion in Rome. However, systemic problems did arise because the Christians and Jews by virtue of allegiance to their God would not fulfill the basic duty of bowing down to idols or calling the emperor "lord." "To the Christians, the essence of the Lord was in the One and only Lord Jesus Christ who had come as ruler of the world."[7] The Romans perceived Christian allegiance as a direct disregard for the laws of the entire Roman Empire and blatant rejection of a formal requirement of the state. Not knowing how to deal with the rebellion immediately, this became a major concern for the Romans. Within a short period of time, this problem was exacerbated because small Christian communities began to spring up in all the main centers of the Roman Empire and beyond the Roman frontiers, and none of these communities were dedicated to the Roman state religion. Complicating matters, the Christians' referring to the Lord Jesus Christ as "Lord" and the untimely burning of a great part of Rome during Nero's reign raised many serious questions about the Christians, which lead to the beginning of serious Christian persecution.

"Although there were periodic lulls in Christian persecution by the Romans, during the beginning of the Second Century, under Emperor Trajan, Christianity itself was a crime and anyone associated with Christian thought would be punished and no less put to death. Subsequently, for more than three centuries, the Roman Empire adopted a hostile attitude towards Christianity, which varied from indifference to scornful toleration to outright violent persecution."[8] It was not until Constantine's time did the church have anyone to deal with persecutions, schisms, and heresies. According to James H. Rutz, "Until Constantine there was no such thing as a church building or 'Christian' architecture. A church building had never been dreamed of in a dream. That which we know as the Christian faith was a living room movement! The Christian faith was the first and only religion ever to exist that did use special temples of worship. It is the only living room religion in human history."[9]

The division of the Roman Empire into eastern and western geographic areas took place largely during the third century. Despite each sector having its own governor, the Roman Empire theoretically still functioned as one empire. As stated earlier, this separation came about for a variety of political, linguistic, social, and theological reasons, many of which have yet to be resolved. For almost five centuries this was a period of some of the greatest theological disputes in church history. In fact, many of these religious differences resurfaced during World War I and II and most definitely in the Bosnia-Yugoslavian war of the 1990s.

With the eventual overpowering involvement and control by the Roman state, the struggle to attain Christian truth became very complicated. "Religion was primarily a state matter because the state itself was a divine establishment, a divine form of human society."[10] This meant that "the theocratic nature of the state was such that it believed that freedom was granted so the divinity abiding in the heavens might be mercifully and favorably inclined towards the state and to all who were under state authority."[11] Constantine saw things differently. The more he became aware of Christianity, the more hostile he became toward paganism. Enriched by the Christian mindset, Constantine's overall plan was to unify the empire, and he felt that unity could only come about if the unity was based on spiritual and religious elements. Thus, unity of the empire became a major political factor for Constantine, as well as for his successors who made every effort to enforce it.

Although Constantine's desire for Roman unity never materialized, during his reign, Constantine began to consider himself both a lawgiver of the Eastern Empire and a Christian. Constantine would not combine Christianity with pagan falsehoods, nor did he feel that the ambiguous union of two faiths, paganism and the Christianity, could coexist. Subsequently, Constantine's hostile stance toward paganism eventually decided the fate of the church in newborn Byzantium. It was during this time that the theocratic paganism of Rome was doomed to ruin.

Even with the rise of the Orthodox Church, Donatism, which asserted that sanctity is essential to sacrament, church membership was still able to develop new relations between church and state. But yet to come was the Arian disturbance that took up the whole first century of the age of Constantine. "Arius was a scholarly Alexandrian presbyter and preacher who began to teach that Christ, as the Son of God and one of God's creations, must necessarily be recognized as created in time, since his birth could take place only in time. He had been born of God as an instrument for the creation of the world, and therefore, 'there was a time when He was not.' Consequently, the Son of God was wholly distinct from the Father and not equal to Him."[12] This school of thought set the church apart for a period of fifty years at a time when to be a Christian was literally a matter of life and death. This is exactly why Christians today need to stay apprised of political winds in all corners of the world and get involved in the fight against anything that resembles Christian persecution or endeavors for denominational control.

A clear example of the "on guard" policy is seen when the active believers of the church were horrified by Arius' distortion of the sacred principles of the church. As a result, his own bishop, Alexander of Alexandria, censured Arius. Censure, however, was not the answer. Arius continued his quest for recognition of his belief, which ultimately brought governmental authorities to his side, enhancing the creation of an intellectual class with the church eager for rational explanation of the faith. Subsequently, the Arian heresy began to spread throughout the East. But with Emperor Constantine's intervention, "the union of Emperor and Empire was fastly becoming instruments for the kingdom of Christ. The dream of extending Christianity throughout the world was encouraged and enhanced by a group of unofficial Christian counselors who centered on Constantine. The first was Eusebius of Nicomedia"[13]

Although Constantine could not fully understand the essence of Arius' theological dispute, he was disturbed by the new dissension within the church. To counter the Arian movement, Constantine called the First Ecumenical Council, which took place in Nicaea in the spring of 324. It was here that the prelates from all parts of the church had gathered and renewed the confirmation that Christ was once again victorious over the world.

Although Arius' theological perspective was almost unanimously condemned, a new argument arose. "At the Council of Nicaea the term homoousion - of the substance was introduced. This term describes a precise definition of the relationship of the Son to the Father, by calling the Son "consubstantial" (homoousion) with the Father, and consequently equal to Him in divinity. This term was so precise as to exclude any possibility of reinterpretation, Arianism was no longer considered."[14] A small group of bold, farsighted theologians, however, did not accept the mere condemnation of Arius and sought to crystallize church tradition into a clear concept. The main concern by the theologians was the word homoousion, because for the first time, a creedal definition had been made to contain a term alien to the Scripture. At the request of Constantine, the word homoousion remained as a dignified symbol of faith without having to probe into the ramification of its meaning. Constantine did not live to see his thirst for establishing a semblance of heavenly truth and beauty on earth. He died on Pentecost in the year 337. The story goes that upon his deathbed Constantine was the first Roman emperor to actually embrace the Christian faith.

"So great was Constantine's power and influence, he was buried in the midst of the sarcophagi of the twelve disciples, six on the right and six on the left. Those sarcophagi contained relics of the apostles, and thus almost equated him with the Redeemer Himself."[15] Although his brilliancy was acknowledged and written as such, the expression for the level of that brilliancy should not be accepted as a comparison to or almost equal to Christ. Extreme reverence does have its place but not when it comes to using Christ as the measure of relative significance.

Bolstering Constantine's image and legacy was Eusebius of Caesarea, "who was the court theologian of Constantine the Great. [He] proclaimed that Constantine had a direct relationship with God and was evidenced merely by the fact that God had not sent other men to instruct him but had personally guided the emperor by inspiration and miraculous heavenly visions."[16] Eusebius' portrait of Constantine had elevated him as both political and sacramental heir to Roman god-emperor. However history views Constantine's contributions, we must never forget that before Constantine's time the church had had to deal with schisms and heresies by relying solely upon its own resources.

> Despite the fickle and frequently superficial judgment of Constantine by historians, Constantine had an unwavering thirst for God and made decisions which ultimately led to the triumphancy and world-wide recognition of Eastern Orthodoxy. Constantine encouraged the separation of the Roman Empire and strengthened his position when he founded a second capital in the east alongside Old Rome in Italy. For Eastern Christianity, Constantine was and remains the initiator of the Orthodox Christian world, which ultimately became the crown for the heroic feats of the martyrs. The West, on the other hand, tends to view the era of Constantine as the beginning of enslavement of the Church by the State and the falling away of the Church at its height of primitive Christian freedom.[17]

Because the Eastern Orthodox Church believes that no priest is an intercessor between human beings and God and that Jesus Christ is the head of the church and not a selected man, the aforementioned comment made by the West could be expected. In fact, Jesus' role as head of the church is supported in Colossians 1:18. Paul says, "And He is the head of the body, the church: who is the beginning, the firstborn from the dead; that in all things he might have the preeminence."[18] Despite his successes, after Constantine's death Orthodox Christendom became more and more difficult to maintain.

By the end of the third century, persecutions of Christians increased. But during this time, the Roman Empire began to crumble. There were attacks by Germanic tribes from the north and the Goths and Persians from the east. The leaders' failures related to these attacks made it an opportune time to look for scapegoats, so why not blame the Christians?

Subsequently, it was during this period that persecuting Christians reached its highest point.

As with many other periods in the development of Eastern Orthodoxy, as part of the Islamic drive to conquer the world, the seventh century Arab Muslim rule of Alexandria, Antioch, and Jerusalem also curtailed and weakened the growth of Orthodox Christianity. "At first, the Muslim world was somewhat tolerant of Christians but towards the end of the Turkish reign it been said that there was not very much pity towards the state of Orthodoxy. In fact, one of the greatest catastrophes in the history of Christianity by Islamic domination was the capture and sacking of Constantinople by the armies of Mohammed II in 1453."[19] This meant that the Ottoman Empire, excepting Moscow, Russia, now embraced the whole of the Christian East. Orthodoxy under the Turks felt itself on the defensive, making survival their greatest aim. The goal was to keep things going in hope of better days to come. Persecutions began, and "out of 159 Patriarchs, who have held office between the fifteenth and the twentieth century, the Turks have on 105 occasions driven Patriarchs from their throne; there have been 27 abdications, often involuntarily; 6 Patriarchs have suffered death by hanging, poisoning, or drowning; and only 21 have died natural causes while in office."[20]

As one could guess, there was very little ecclesiastical education during the period of Turkish rule. With a historical policy of wholesale strangulation of Christianity, in general, it is a wonder Eastern Orthodoxy as a separate church managed to survive. This is exactly why Christians should not take their religious preference too lightly. Today, Christians are being attacked from every which way imaginable, making each and every Christian morally liable for defending Christian doctrines. If Christians don't, who will?

On the historical and developmental road of Orthodoxy, the Russian chapter is one of the more recent. "In Russia there was independence from Byzantium, liberation from Turkey in 1877, Muscovite domination of the Church, discrepancies between conservatism and ritualism, and the ultimate triumph of Bolshevism. Communism did very little to enhance the growth of the Orthodox Church. The communists managed to control the Church by building a society in which there would no longer be any place for a Church."[21] This was accomplished by "excluding the Church from all social or charitable work and from any part in education. Atheist propaganda was also instrumental in disallowing the Church from reaching the youth of Russia."[22] These exact political tools are evidenced today.

It is said that the Bolshevik Revolution in Russia in 1917 and the years between the two world wars inflicted sufferings upon Christians that were equal in cruelty to those endured by the earliest Christians. If we were to compare Bolshevik history with today, we would see great similarities in how the U.S. government wants to take away the charitable efforts of the church and have the people rely more on government. All this and more is happening under the mantra of "change." More damaging is the elimination of school prayer that disallows the church from reaching the youth of the country. As much of the world struggles toward freedom, America struggles to keep hers.

In conjunction with the butchery of millions of its citizens, "in 1918 and 1919 alone, about twenty-eight bishops alone were killed; between 1923 and 1926 some fifty more were murdered by the Bolsheviks. Parish clergy and monks also suffered severely: by 1926, according to information supplied by a bishop living in Russia at the time, some 2,700 priests, 2000 monks, and 3,400 nuns and other ordained persons had been killed."[23] This may be old information for some, but the wars in Yugoslavia in the 1990s were said to have started because of the wholesale slaughter of Orthodox priests and nuns by the Roman Catholic and Muslim Croats. In addition, there were hundreds of Orthodox churches that were burned and bombed, as well as centuries-old monasteries and their ancient frescos. All this was going on while the UN silently stood by and watched.

Not to minimize Russian communist repression of Eastern Orthodox churches, but for political reasons there was no wholesale closure of churches. In addition, "recalcitrant clergy who had been imprisoned were not always necessarily put to death. The Communists eventually discovered that martyrdom only makes more stubborn."[24] Under Joseph Stalin, however, communism was committed by its fundamental principles to an aggressive and militant atheism. Communism did not merely stop with separation of church and state. It sought either by direct or indirect means to overcome all organized church life or to extirpate all religious belief. With the destruction of modern-day communism, however, and with the help of Christian evangelists, Eastern Christian Orthodoxy in Russia is now on the rise, and Russia's people are hungry once again for the Orthodox Christianity they once knew.

With the geographical division of the Roman Empire and the breakdown of communication, we can look to two primary factors that kept the two main churches from remaining as one. First, the West was guilty of asserting papal infallibility, and secondly, the West spread their own interpretations of doctrines on the Holy Spirit and the immaculate conception of the Virgin Mary. The Orthodox Church viewed both aspects as contradictory to the basic truths of Christian theology that were already resolved at the Council meetings at Nicaea. While not all-inclusive, the Orthodox Church views the ideas of eternal punishment being resolved in a geographical place called purgatory and some of the differences concerning the contents of the Nicene Creed as lying in Arianism.

More than likely we will never know the answers to any of the theological pragmatics even when we make the transition to the "other side." Who knows, maybe heaven and hell reside in one's head, and it is simply how each domain is viewed that determines your relationship to God. Respectfully, if this is the case, it is your interpretation of heaven and hell that will either tie you to Christ or push you to the "dark side."

The past few sentences were not intended to condemn but to show both sides of the theological argument. However, it is only right to add that gaining knowledge of the world does not necessarily mean better control of one's environment. This is especially true when the psychology of living tends to get in the way of healthy reasoning. We see evidence for this shortfall in the garden incident; as well in most everything man endeavors to do.

The oddity of the church separation is that the early wholesale unity of the church was viewed as Jesus coming to gather the children of God into one. Paul implied this when he wrote, "There is neither Jew nor Greek, there is neither bond nor free, there is neither male nor female: for ye all are one in Jesus Christ."[25] To me what this says is there were motivations other than doctrinal differences of Christ that brought the schism to a head.

As if the separation of the church was not enough to contend with, the Western church was also beginning to get bogged down in many complex problems; including a defensive attack against certain Roman Catholic practices by a German monk named Martin Luther. In 1517 Luther nailed his list of Ninety-five Theses to a church door in Wittenberg signaling the start of what came to be known as the Protestant Reformation. Although Luther's initial intent was not to break away from the Church of Rome, he wanted to change the papal system of government as well as other doctrinal issues. But as a result, Luther was excommunicated in 1521. This only exacerbated the already troubled unity of the Western church.

According to Rutz, Luther could not have done what he did without the help of "Frederick the Wise, alias Frederick III who just happened to command the largest army in Europe and he was royally peeved because he had not been made Pope."[26] Under Frederick's warning, at all costs, Luther was protected. Complicating matters, religious radicals on all frontiers of the Roman Catholic Church and Protestant movement began to surface claiming not to be either Protestant or Roman Catholic. Thus, the ecclesiastical monopoly to which the Western church was accustomed had greatly diminished. This was not a peaceful time for the Roman Catholic Church. Radicals took advantage of the internal strife and went on a rampage burning countless churches and destroying icons and precious frescos. In retrospect, this was not Luther's original intent.

With Christendom divided into two halves, their own doing hampered the efforts of both the East and the West. "The Eastern Church claiming to be the only true Church of Christ, it saw its hopeful theological, doctrinal, cultural, and geographical endeavors restricted by identifying strictly with the Byzantine world. The church of the East also felt that the church of the West had lost its doctrinal and ecclesiological balance of primitive Christianity and this lack of balance was ultimately for provoking the reaction of the sixth century, the Protestant Reformation."[27]

Long before the Protestant Reformation, "when Paul and other apostles traveled around the world, the Roman Empire was a rather closely knit political and culturally unified Empire. There were many different national groups with dialects and languages but were still governed by one emperor. But in the centuries that followed, the unity of the Roman Empire divided geographically with the Mediterranean being first to experience internal strife. Despite the theological perspective of being one, the political unity of the Greek east and the Latin west was destroyed by the barbarian invasions and never permanently restored."[28] The eventual rise of Islam helped to split the church even more.

Moving forward:

> Two hundred fifty years before the glowing distinction between the East and the West theological doctrine, the Pope crowned Charles the Great, King of the Franks, as emperor. Charlemagne sought recognition from the ruler of Byzantium, but without success. The Byzantines still adhering to the principles of imperial unity regarded Charlemagne as an intruder and the Papal coronation as an act of schism within the empire. Thus, with the creation of the Holy Roman Empire in the west, instead of drawing Europe closer together, only served to alienate east and west more than [ever] before.[29]

The individual primary language of the two sectors further complicated matters.

When we look at all the complexities and the long history of martyrdom of the Orthodox Church, no one particular event completely shaped the Orthodox Church of today. "Its history is deeply entrenched in a conglomeration of events, people, places, and times which ultimately led to the semi-antithetical opinion of the Western Catholic Christian Church. Above all, [Orthodoxy] still maintains that all Christians must return to one true faith, the faith of the first ecumenical councils, as the condition for true reunion."[30] But as with the different factions of Islam, this unity does not seem foreseeable any time soon.

While there have been many meetings and councils throughout Christian history, there are seven great ecumenical councils that the Orthodox Church recognizes.

> Nicaea in 325, Constantinople in 381, Ephesus in 431, Chalcedon in 451, Constantinople II in 553, Constantinople III in 680, and Nicaea II in 785. In 325, the first council had condemned Arius and defined the incarnate Son of God as "consubstantial" with the Father. The Second council had spent some time in putting the Arius issue to rest and developing what is known as the Nicaean-Constantinople Creed. In 431, the Third council had condemned Nestorianism and declared that there were not two persons existing side by side in Christ-God and a man called Jesus but the divinity and humanity were united in one person. Consequently, Mary, the Mother of Jesus, is the mother of God.[31]

> The fourth council affirmed that the Son of God must be confessed in two natures unconfused, immutably, indivisibly, inseparably, and united in one person. At the Fifth council, which essentially is the Second Counsel of Constantinople, Emperor Justinian wished to prove that the Fourth council had not fallen into Nestorianism [which implies that divine and human persons remained separate in the incarnate Christ]. As a result, three theologians suspected of Nestorian views were put to death. During the third council of Constantinople, the council maintained that the humanity is not an abstract entity in Christ but is manifested by its own will, subject freely and in all things to the divine will. Christ, therefore, has two wills.[32]

Finally, the Second Council of Nicaea defined the Orthodox doctrine concerning the images of Christ and the saints. It was felt that because the Word of God was truly incarnate and true man, then He must be represented pictorially. Although seemingly dogmatic, the councils were not purely limited to questions and answers related to dogma. The Orthodox Church's constitutional and administrative organization was also settled during this time.

Although small in numbers compared to Western Catholicism, the legendary beauty of the Orthodox Church seems to be on the rise and on its way to worldwide resurgence, especially with the restructuring of full-blown communism in Russia. Rejecting such things as Rome's ecclesiastical hierarchy and the concept of the infallibility of a man designated as pope, the Eastern Church has been able to maintain its identity without compromising its duty as legatee of what it believes to be the tradition and teachings given to the twelve apostles by Christ.

Now, one would think with such resilience why is there a need to worry about present-day persecutions? The truth of the matter is that past persecutions did not necessary begin by one major onslaught; as Rutz puts it, "Rome wasn't unbuilt in a day."[33] It was over a period of time that the true doctrine began to erode away by those in the formal church who held differences of opinion as to how the Christian doctrine was to be presented. Thus, the external and internal discrepancies outlined in this chapter should not be taken lightly because in many ways paganism and anti-Christian sentiment is on the rise. Specific contributing factors are satanic cults, the use of crystals, self-proclaimed prophets, and many other diverse schools of thought far from the guiding principles of Christ.

Bringing this chapter to a close you'll remember that in the opening statement I gave attention to Christian persecutions and how they are no different today as they were then. My observation, of course, is not the single most. In Rutz's book he quotes Dr. E. M. Blaiklock, Professor of Classics at Auckland University in New Zealand who once said, "Of all the centuries, the twentieth is most like the first."[34] How profound and yet so much on the back burner in the scheme of things. In the short run, to make Christianity work and remain respectful, it all goes back to personal responsibility and accountability.

Now that you've read this fast-track piece of early church history, you might ask yourself what you could personally do to ward off Christian persecution so you too could avoid having to ask, can present day Christianity survive without compromising its truths to accommodate man's continual fall?

III

MODERN-DAY RELIGIOUS WARFARE

Chapter two was a brief presentation on some of the earliest church strife between the two Catholic Christian populations. To show how dissension between these two groups is far from over, this chapter discusses some of the specifics of the modern-day Bosnian war. When I am finished, you will come to realize that the war in Bosnia may have been one of genocide but not by those who the media portrayed as the perpetrators. Within the following pages, the real perpetrator will be uncovered through the employment of truths that the biased, government-controlled media refused to reveal.

Given the structural content of the book, this chapter is necessary for two reasons. First, it is relevant to the Christian persecutory theme, and it is a classic example of the many tribulations Christian denominationalism causes. Secondly, the chapter reveals how political chicanery and the media did influence outcomes through one-sided propaganda, making the Serbians the culprit. Specifically, supported by Germany and the United States, the media became an arm for the Roman Catholic Croatian Army and Croatian Police. Serbia's European enemies had "engaged Ruder Finn, an American Public Relations firm, to get their message out."[1] Because of sanctions, the Serbian Orthodox Christians lost the public relations war. Thus, the news was presented in such a way that it favored a particular contrived political view for those who obviously had a vested interest in outcomes-namely Germany, Serbia's enemy during World War I and World War II. The recent leftist Hollywood presentation of this war is ever more distorted. But just because the news no longer covers the ethnic and religious problems related to this war, it does not mean the long-held hatred has disappeared. It is merely on slow burn and, for several political, social, and economic reasons, may well be the procuring cause for World War III.

Where to begin is not easy because to this day this region has a lengthy history of unresolved geographical, religious, constitutional, and political parliamentary disputes. Given this history, these differences reached their boiling point when the killing of Orthodox priests and nuns by the Croatian Roman Catholics and the Muslims was discovered, "making revenge by the Serbians, under these circumstances, the most logical step. Furthermore, on a much broader scale, according to T.W. Carr, associate publisher of *Defense and Foreign Affairs' Strategic Policy*, the war largely began with the help of Germany because of its historical objective to control the territories of Croatia, Slovenia, and Dalmatia, with their access to the Adriatic and Mediterranean."[2]

Above and beyond all the propagandized reports against Serbia, the irony of this war is that it was largely Roman Catholic Christians killing Orthodox Christians with both groups simultaneously turning on the Muslims. We must remind ourselves that Croatia was a World War II ally of Germany, and, for political reasons, Marshal Tito was supported by the United States during that time. Another example of political chicanery is seen in how the world in the 1990s, including the United States, stood by and watched hundreds of thousands of Christians and animists being slaughtered by the Arab Muslims in Sudan. Because the United States and the rest of the world did not have a vested interest within this region, the world did not intervene. The only answer to this atrocity is that the political and religious privities tied to such a travesty are found in the appeasement of Islam to maintain the flow of oil. The problem is this situation is currently getting worse and could very well end up being another religious war between radical Islam and Roman Catholicism.

Rather than immediately focusing on the early days of tribal warfare I will begin with a more recent history of the Bosnian War. Again, I have to remind you that the world's general consensus about this war came from a politically motivated, one-sided media. Staying true to form, today's media has not lost its fervor for protecting the ineptness and corruption of political figures all the way up to the president. Given how the various arms of government and the media handle national and international political crises, I feel comfortable in saying Christianity needs to stay on its toes and pay attention to the worldwide political chessboard.

From its very beginning, Yugoslavia has been inundated with cultural, geographical, religious, linguistic, and economic hates and differences that have their roots in long held but not exclusively tribal warfare. This accounts for why the Orthodox religion in many parts of the world still suffers persecution to this day. A long time in the making, some of the issues that contributed to the tumultuous state of the Balkan-Yugoslavian region came with the collapse of the Ottoman Empire that ultimately tore apart Orthodox Byzantium and brought about the eventual fall of the Habsburg monarchy, the Balkan Wars, World War I, and World War II. Assuredly, in the near future this volatile geographical area will more than likely play a crucial role in World War III, which will once again be a license for revisiting old and ingrained hatreds.

During the World War II, in order to have a better idea as to what was taking place in the Baltic region, the allied forces sent an envoy to Yugoslavia to find out who was fighting against and killing the most Nazis: was it General Mihaijlovic of the Serbian Chetnik Army, which was a faction of Serbian irregular forces loyal to the exiled king, or Marshal Tito, who directed the communist, partisan Croatian Ustasha? Far from overstated, the indigenous various peoples of Yugoslavia viewed the war as an opportune time for settling ancient ethnic tribal, political, and religious differences by massacring one another; the most inhumane butchery ever in recorded human history was done by the Roman Catholic Croatian Ustasha and with the approval of the Vatican. Mind you, this was Christian against Christian.

Evidence for these atrocities can be found in the book *Convert ... or Die* by Edmond Paris. He presents documented facts that (as an inconspicuous fan of Nazi Germany) "the Roman Catholic Church was instrumental in liquidating over 800,000 Orthodox Serbians in Croatia, Yugoslavia, during the years 1940-1945."[3] Aside from Paris' report, other sources say that, many of these atrocities were committed in some of the most brutal ways: "250 peasants buried alive in the Serbian district of Bjelovar";[4] "2000 children gassed in the death camp at Bosanska Gradiska";[5] "a father and son crucified together and then burned in their own home in Mliniste";[6] "mothers and children impaled on the same stake";[7] "a mother forced to hold the basin which caught the blood of her four sons as their throats were slit in Kosinj";[8] "an expectant mother having her unborn child cut from her womb and replaced by a cat in the death camp at Jasenovac";[9] "1,360 prisoners having their throats cut in a single night by one guard during a sadistic throat-cutting contest (also at Jasenovac)";[10] "not to mention dismemberments";[11] "'graviso knives' for specialized throat cutting";[12] "necklaces of human tongues and eyes";[13] "the confining of prisoners to rooms filled with blood to the ankles";[14] "and ten thousand other atrocities condoned by the Roman Catholic Archbishop Aloysius Stepinac-the church's version of Adolph Eichmann-who prayed at the opening of the Croatian Parliament in February of 1942, for ... the Holy Ghost to descend upon the sharp knives of the Ustashi (Catholic guerrilla army)."[15] It was not until a German Nazi commander wrote to his superiors about the butcheries of the Ustasha that the macabre killings ceased. Beyond the physical atrocities, many Serbian Orthodox Christians were forced into converting to Roman Catholicism.

No doubt, the Serbian Army did their fair share of citizen butchery, which could have been worse had they not been preoccupied with fighting the Nazis, the Hungarian and Bulgarian German sympathizers, and the Axis Italians all at the same time. The Serbian Orthodox Chetniks were also helping the Jews escape and saving American pilots who were shot down over enemy territory. They rarely surrendered the whereabouts of a pilot, and, as a result, whole villages were slaughtered.

What could anyone possibly gain from the remnants of such horror? "General Mihaijlovic [Serbian] promised a rebirth of the Kingdom of Yugoslavia, under Serbian rule. Tito [Croatian] promised a new federal Yugoslavia, national equality, and a dramatic change in the prewar sociopolitical order. Tito called for an all-out war against fascism, with the victory of communism as the ultimate goal. Mihaijlovic called for the defense of the Serbian nation and the defeat of Communism."[16] History reflects that at war's end, despite Tito's revolutionary objectives, for reasons far, far too complicated to mention, the Allied powers overwhelmingly supported Tito's Partisans. This move, however, eventually proved to cause havoc in modern-day Kosovo because Tito rewarded his military supporters with high political positions, which made it easier to turn against Serbian citizens. More disturbing, Mihaijlovic, the general who is credited with saving hundreds of American pilots, was executed by Tito after the war.

Winning his personal war against the Chetnik, Tito became the ultimate dominant force in Yugoslavia. Once in power, he set out to "communize" Yugoslavia into six federal republics and two autonomous provinces-Kosova and Vojvodina. The problem is some of the geographical dividing lines cut in half different provinces, leaving various ethnic groups stranded in what appeared to be foreign territory. This was also problematic for Clinton's Vance-Owens Peace Plan because it meant relocating thousands of people.

To his credit, irrespective of all the ethnic and religious differences within Yugoslavia, Tito managed to keep a resemblance of solidarity. But after his death in 1980, Yugoslavia would remain stable for only ten more years. The stability of Yugoslavia formally ceased in September 1990 when Serb-Muslim clashes occurred in the ethnically mixed border town of Foca on the Drina River.

A most important fact in all of this religious and political mayhem is that no one really knows for sure who the first inhabitants of Bosnia were. But historically, the Serbs and Croats settled in the region sometime in the late sixth and early seventh centuries. They appeared first in small tribes but were essentially drawn from a single Slavic confederation-the Slaveni.

The Serbs settled in an area corresponding to what is known
as Rascia and gradually extended their rule to territories
of Dioclea (Montenegro) and Hum (Herzegovina). The
Croats settled in areas roughly corresponding to modern
Croatia, and probably also including most of Bosnia proper.
It is within these regions the Slavs settled in traditional
hierarchical units developed from family units, clans, and
eventually tribes. It was not until the seventh century that
the Byzantine rulers attempted to Christianize the Croats
using Latin priests and the remote areas of Bosnia were
the last to undergo the process of being Christianized.[17]

By 1463, the Muslims were entrenched in Bosnia with the various
cultural Bosnian peasants becoming the sharecroppers for Muslim
landlords. It was also at this point that the Ottoman invasion forced the
Bosnian Roman Catholics and the Orthodox Slavs to accept and adopt the
religion of their foreign invaders and conquerors, converting them to Islam.
As a result, the majority of Bosnian Muslims today are Serbo-Croatian
speaking converts. From one generation to the next, the politics, language,
and religion of this area remain strained and pertinent to the causes for
the ensuing war. When the Ottoman Turks began to expand their territory
westward, they did so at the expense of their Orthodox Christian neighbors.
The ultimate goal was to master the Balkan Peninsula. Through rape,
plunder, and conquest, the Ottomans tore apart the Orthodox Byzantium.
This was the last remnant of the Eastern Roman Empire torn by centuries
of Western Roman Catholic crusaders.
Even by today's model:

It is difficult to verify and discern who the original
inhabitants of Bosnia may have been because there are
several different languages and culture within more
than a thousand years of history. By today's standard,
the modern population of Bosnia can properly be called
Slav with the Bosnian territory itself having been under
several different invaders and conquerors. For instance,
in the tenth century, Bosnia was briefly part of the short-
lived Serbian State of Caslav; after Caslav died in battle
in about 960, much of Bosnia was briefly incorporated
into the Croatian State of Kresimer II; soon thereafter in
about 997 Samuel of Bulgaria marched through Bosnia
and well asserted his overlordship over parts of Bosnia.
After the Byzantines defeated Samuel and annexed
Bulgaria in 1018, Byzantine asserted its suzerainty over

Bosnia; this lasted until later in the century, when some
of Bosnia was incorporated into Croatia and some into
Duklja (basically modern Montenegro). In 1137 Hungry
annexed most all of Bosnia, only to lose it to the Byzantine
Empire in 1167. Soon in 1180, Hungry reasserted itself
and by treaty regained its suzerainty over Bosnia. Prior
to 1180 parts of Bosnia were briefly found in Serb and
Croats units but neither of these groups had held Bosnia
long enough to acquire their loyalty or to impose serious
claim to Bosnia.[18]

With such diversification one can understand why something as simple
as blended families have so much difficulty with "his and hers children."
It was a multifaceted environment:

From the 620's and the emergence of an independent
Bosnia state in the 1180's, no simple conclusions could
be drawn. Bosnia's proper was under Serb rule at times:
above all, in the mid-tenth century and at the end of the
eleventh. However, it would be misleading to say that
Bosnia was ever a geographical part of Serbia because
although Herzegovina was clearly a Serb territory,
Bosnia's proper was aligned towards the Croat-Hungarian
cultural and political realm. In addition, Bosnia's religious
organization during its early medieval period was linked
more towards Croatia and not towards Serbian lands.[19]

Subsequently, the plight of these unresolved territorial issues had
never been formally finalized until modern-day Germany got its hand in
the mix. Specifically, although the European community agreed the best
way to avoid a modern-day war in Yugoslavia was to allow Yugoslavia to
remain one nation, "during the protracted negotiations, Germany wore
down the European Community members and eventually, at 0400 hours on
the morning of the debate, the 11:1 vote to hold Yugoslavia united turned
into a unanimous [one] vote to recognize Croatia as an independent state
on the grounds that the right to self-determination overruled all other
criteria."[20] This move made it one step closer to all-out war.

Given all the variables of the Bosnian region, the 1990s saw Yugoslavia
in a state of crisis most every day. Genocide and "ethnic cleaning" had
become the buzzwords of the five o'clock news. The problem was the "buzz
words" were referenced to the wrong side. From an article written by
Richard Palmer in the Philadelphia Trumpet he states that Krauthammer
wrote in *Time*, April 5, 1999, that "investigators with the war-crimes tribunal

in Hague have concluded that this campaign [genocide] was carried out with brutality, wanton murder, and indiscriminate shelling of civilians ... the massacre Krauthammer was describing occurred in the region of Karin in Croatia. Croatian troops forced an estimated 200,000 Serbs to flee."[21] The massacre Krauthammer was referring to was cited in the National Post, March 13, 2004. The same article addresses that although Croatians invited the Serbs to return, Orthodox Serbians were continually murdered, their homes burned, and their lands were confiscated.

Given its lengthy history, it was inevitable that the long-held historical strife in this region would eventually turn into was, but modern-day politics certainly is guilty of consuming and fueling its probable cause. This is not to say that genuine efforts were not made to make peace in the region. In its seventy years of existence as a state, efforts to maintain solidarity in Yugoslavia were in the form of monarchy, communism, and centralized and decentralized government, but in the end, the best each could offer was temporary conciliatory cooperation and peace. Adding to the modern-day strife were the never-reconciled issues from the earlier division of the Roman Empire with its established fault lines between Western and Eastern political, religious, and ethnic populations. To this very day the three major religions of Eastern Orthodoxy, Roman Catholicism, and Islam still remain the dividing line between Yugoslavia's solidarity. Once more, the media never did address this as a religious war, and for political reasons it was most often one-sided reporting with the Serbian Orthodox Christians continuously portrayed as the villain. As evidenced by Deuteronomy 16:19, in this matter the press was guilty of heresy. "Thou shalt not wrest judgment; thou shall not respect persons, neither take a gift: for a gift doth blind the eyes of the wise, and pervert the words of the righteous."[22]

It was not until a three-month study of news reports done by Howard University Professor of International Relations Nikolaos Stavrou that this one-sided pattern of news coverage was detected. Stavrou pointed out, "Most of the stories [presented on the Serbs] were based on hearsay evidence with a few attempts to show 'the other side's perspectives.' Ninety percent of the stories originated in Sarajevo, but only 5 percent in Belgrade ... Stavrou's analysis cited ethnic stereotyping with the Serbs referred to as primitive remnants of the Ottoman Empire and Yugoslav Army officers described as 'orthodox communist generals.' Newspaper photographs neglected to show suffering or dead Serbs or destroyed Serb churches and villages."[23]

A modern-day scenario that illustrates a misrepresentation and projection of blame is that of the Jewish-Palestinian unrest. Each year the Arab world observes what is called Naksa ("setback"), a lamenting for the disastrous efforts of the Arab world to destroy Israel during the

1948 War of Independence and the ensuing defeat in the 1967 Six-Day War. "These marked events are in reality just veiled attempts to de-legitimize the State of Israel-in these cases by portraying Israel as the aggressor and the Palestinians as helpless 'refugees' whom they wrongly say Israelis drove from their land when Israel was established. To call these protestors 'refugees' is, however, beyond imagination since most have never lived or set foot in Israel. They are the descendants of Arabs who left Palestine by their own free will, in spite of Israel's offers for them to stay and help build a new nation together."[24]

Looking for ways to resolve the Bosnian problem, one group of contemporary political evaluators presented a solution that was predicated on economics because they felt that "the main basis for hostility is not ethnic or religious but economic: the resentment felt by members of a mainly [but not exclusively] Christian peasantry towards their Muslim landowners."[25] How naïve to suggest one probable cause for a ravaged region rooted in identifiable ancient tribal warfare and religious and language differences. Let us not forget the cultural and political influences of the ancient and historical empires of Rome, Charlemagne, Ottoman and Austria-Hungary.

Another radical position concerning the Bosnian turmoil is "the belief that the war in Yugoslavia broke out against a background of sea change in Europe, framed on one side by the collapse of the Soviet Union and the Eastern Bloc and on the other side by the movement of unification of Western Europe."[26] No doubt the religious-genocide war in Yugoslavia is in part a reflection of these changes and a clue to possible future events. One cannot help think that with the 1918 development of the Yugoslavian state, instead of homogenization, the enlargement of Yugoslavia caused even deeper ethnic disunity.

In part, the aforementioned geographical changes are also to blame for the uneven national development, which impaired the longtime unrealistic goal of Yugoslavia's one nation housed in a one-state concept. Through every aspect of trial and error, there is no getting away from the fact that Yugoslavia's birth as a nation in 1918 began in the chaos and blood of World War I. Foremost, because of a multicultural environment, which utilizes two alphabets, three religious faiths, three main languages, and numerous other tongues, and despite centuries of trying, these differences as a whole contribute to why the Western European countries have not been able to deal with the Balkans with much success.

Jockeying for supremacy, the push between these opposing forces was beginning to be more like a shove. "The beginning of the 1990's proved no less troubling when the threats of war and calls for succession by the former Yugoslavian Republics led to the collapse of the State and to horrific fighting not seen in Europe for generations."[27] Although the demise of Yugoslavia was expected, it was formally forewarned in December 1990 when the *New York Times* carried the news of a Central Intelligence Agency report predicting that "Yugoslavia would fall apart in eighteen months because of ethnic tensions and political fighting among the Republics."[28] The report warned that civil war was possible. Despite such a warning, no major powers gave much credence to the pending bloodshed or the political and geographical break up of Yugoslavia. But then again, maybe world opinion wanted to see how everything played out before intervening, which would justify and give credibility to self-serving positions.

Always festering to the boiling point, modern-day provocation occurred because "during World War II, Bosnia-Herzegovina became an integral part of the collaborationist Independent State of Croatia. With that came harsh systematic repression by the German-backed Roman Catholic Croatian Ustasha against all Orthodox Serbians in Bosnia. The Ustasha sought to implicate the Muslims in their anti-Serb campaign by frequently wearing fezzes and calling one another by Muslim names. It was determined that the Ustasha was seeking to poison relations for the Muslims with the Serbs."[29]

World War II, however, was not always dominated by Croatia because "during the summer of 1941, the Serbian Chetnik's increasingly gained control over Serb insurgents and carried out gruesome crimes against Muslims of Eastern Bosnia-Herzegovina. There was a mindset by the Chetnik's to cleanse everything of Bosnia that was not Serb."[30] At times such as these:

> It is difficult to estimate the number of Muslim victims of this original 'ethnic cleaning' but it could be counted in the tens of thousands. Bosnia Muslims alone lost 86,000 people during the war or 6.8 per cent of their population mainly to Chetnik terror. Between the late 1940's and early 1960's, the Serb dominance in Bosnia enforced the notion that the Muslims must declare themselves as either Serbian or Croatian thus pushing back the idea of their separate national identity. Bosnia's identity as an independent state, however, finally came on Aril 7, 1992—the fifty-first anniversary of the day Belgrade was leveled by Hitler's bombardment.[31]

Although the modern-day move to declare an independent state for Bosnia was celebrated by the Bosnian Muslims, Radon Karadzic felt this was a direct "violation of the Bosnian constitutional principle requiring consent of all three Bosnian nations in far-reaching decisions such as succession. Essentially, the European community effectively delivered

Radon Karadzic, the self-proclaimed president of Serb Republic of Bosnia-Herzegovina, a pretext for war. Karadzic's argument was that foreign powers, in a familiar historical pattern, were standing in the way of Serb self-determination."[32] As one could expect, this argument convinced many Serbs in Bosnia that the coming war was legitimate and just. Prior to Bosnia's proclamation of wanting sovereignty, Karadzic told foreign journalists, "If Bosnian Muslims persisted in demanding secession from Yugoslavia; you'll see blood up to the knees."[33] The war fulfilled Karadzic's prophecy.

The escalation and atrocities of this war in lives and property are incomprehensible.

> According to the Islamic community, between April and August 1992 alone, Serb extremists destroyed no less than 430 Mosques. This tactic was an effort by Serbian irregulars aimed at adding pressure on the local Muslims to leave the area. Many Muslims were dismissed from their jobs, many were sent to concentration camps, many disappeared in the woods, and many were executed. In Banja Luka alone, more than 400 Muslim owned businesses were blown up. Muslims were stripped of all valuables with little protection under the law. Widespread, Muslims began to simply leave everything behind and flee for their lives.[34]

Again, the press circulated throughout the world the one-sided report of the Bosnian War and deliberately chose not to report that the Serbian reprisals only came after Muslim forces under Naser Oric in Srebrenica "engaged in attacks during Orthodox holidays and destroyed villages [Serbian Orthodox] massacring all the inhabitants. This created a degree of hatred that was quite extraordinary in the region."[35] This massacre included every man, woman, and child because it was Oric's belief that, "One cannot be bothered with taking prisoners."[36] In reality, the Croats and Muslims did more than their share of genocidal activity, but by the grace of the media, their atrocities, although reported, were largely skimmed over as an afterthought.

The reality of all-out war began in April 1991 in the historical, picturesque town of Mostar. Intense fighting broke out between the Serbs and Croats. At the time, Mostar was the largest town in Herzegovina and was 35 percent Muslim, 34 percent Croat, and 19 percent Serb. Because Mostar is located on the line of confrontation between Serb and Croat interests, the Croats were looking to eventually make Mostar the capital of their own ministate, especially since Mostar was a Croatian stronghold during World War II. Thus, in 1991, Mostar became the home of the most extreme Croat nationalists, which forced the Serbs to insist that Mostar belonged to the Republic of Serbia. As could be expected, bitter fighting between the Croats and Serbs followed.

> Croatia was able to achieve its goals in Bosnia-Herzegovina with 'relative discretion' and 'without 'provoking scandals' owing to two sets of circumstances. One, the tolerance shown between the Western Media for Croatia as a 'democratic country' enjoying German support, that is, a country where democratic elections had been held-its flagrant violations of democratic rights not withstanding. The second circumstance provoked a thick smoke screen for Croatian advances. With this international perspective fully in place, Mate Boban, a major gun dealer in Croatia began ruling and expelling Serbs from areas considered Croat ethnic territory.[37]

One of the most bizarre events of the Bosnian War was that before the Croats got a firm hold on what they deemed as their territory, "it was not uncommon for Serbs and Croats to loan each other an artillery piece or tank for the afternoon to be used against the Musilims."[38] Also, odd as it may seem, "Mate Boban and Radovan Karadzic were in regular contact with each other. In early May 1992, they met in Graz, Austria and signed a document outlining how they imagined Bosnia should be divided between them. There was little doubt that both men were acting under the guidance of Tudjman and Milosevic."[39]

The modern-day Bosnian catastrophe was temporarily halted by the first draft of the "Vance-Owen Plan" put together by Cyrus Vance and Lord Owen in October 1992.

> The plan called for reorganization of Bosnia into seven to ten regions with the central government composed of representatives from every region based in Sarajevo. This was found to be unacceptable by the Muslims because the plan did not mention cantons-the small divisions of specific territory. Karadzic was bent on preserving the unity of the Serbian people and wanted to have Bosnia divided into three separate states with each state based on ethnic and religious principles. The Vance-Owen planners rejected this proposition because it meant an uprooting and transporting thousands of people. The Vance-Owen plan broke down on January 30, 1993.[40]

As a result of the breakdown in talks, the Muslims of Bosnia sought military assistance from the United States; the Croatian Army began to attack Serbian-controlled territories near the port of Zadar in Croatia. "In April and May 1993, a full scaled war between the Croats and Muslims raged north and west of Sarajevo, with masked [Roman Catholic] Croats killing Muslims house by house in Vitez and Mostar. And with Serbia's rejection of the Vance-Own plan, the United States planned sanctions on Serbia. This did little to stop the onslaught and grabbing of Muslim territories by both Croatian liberation forces and Serbian Chetniks and irregulars."[41]

Examining the hatred and the religious-political turmoil of this geographical area, it is difficult for spectators to understand the level of hatred held in the crystallized hostilities found in their differences of politics and religion. Supposedly these types of wars ended with the Holy Crusades, but the Bosnian War was no different. Its participants had an unlimited war-like consciousness that carried over into many different arenas. Orthodox Serbians were killing Serbian Muslims; Croatian Roman Catholics were killing Croatian Orthodox and Croatian Muslims; Serbians were killing Croatians of Orthodox faith; and then different groups were siding with each other in an effort to wipe out every Muslim from the face of the earth. In all of this bloodshed, we must never lose sight of the fact that outward expressions of these ongoing hatreds are generally opportunistic, and the territorial and political self-interest of Croatia and Serbia have only been temporarily satisfied. Thus, the likelihood of a military uprising is highly probable. In fact, the Balkan region still has ongoing skirmishes that go unreported by the media.

In closing, there are many ways to compare and look at the Bosnian War, but what stands out the most is the fact that this has been a war based on Christians persecuting Christians with both factions turning on the Muslims. Professing to be civilized, how and why this hatred still stands is even more disturbing. If there is one lesson to learn from all of this is realizing there is nothing ecclesiastical about a leftist media or the souls of self-serving politicians or a zealot religious group. How to avoid the ever present dangers of sectarianism is the question. Where we could safely look is to the grace and wisdom of Scripture because it is never wanting: "And ye shall know the truth, and the truth shall make you free."[42]

IV

JESUS IN THE SCHEME OF THINGS

Evolutionist or otherwise, a wise man would certainly heed the historical relevancy and warnings of Biblical stories and understand that, in most every respect, today's immoral social decadence is not any safer from God's wrath than that of yesteryear. Always wanting yet never learning, human nature decrees reliance on self rather than God. The negative impact of fallout from this arrogance on society has been tremendous. Self-indulgence has turned Biblical histories into nothing more than allegorical stories from long ago. By virtue of this very premise, Biblical history is now viewed as being in the way of the newfound "real purpose and rhythm of life." Blinded by deceit, humans cannot see that God's documented prophecies spelled out in Matthew 24:6-9 have already taken place. Reviewing some of them: "Nation against nation, famine, earthquakes, and you shall be hated for My names sake."[1]

These destructive disasters are not coincidences nor are they merely predetermined consistencies dictated by natural cause. They are a direct result of God trying to get the attention of those who have chosen a path of immorality and thievery while basking in conceit oblivious to their fallibility. Under the umbrella of Christian belief, let's begin to examine the role of Jesus in America's tumultuous state.

First of all, given the appalling immoral state of the general population and public officials, it is quite obvious that behavior in America is completely out of control. So out of control that in many cases, out of control of the very immoral things passed into law that were supposedly for the "highest good" of its citizens. Adding to this runaway freight train of the newfound lifestyle, courts have become reckless in their decision making, and rather than work, America has become a lazy and litigious society hoping to cash in on any legal absurdity that could be conjured- at the same time, wondering why all the jobs are farmed out to foreign countries. Government-induced entitlement programs have taken the place of work, and corporations are thought of as the culprit for all economic disparity. The operant perspective of this conjured politically correct germ has infected the character and integrity of the American people to a point where entitlement rules. Had America not lost a large portion of its God-based mentality, a sense of entitlement would not exist. Satan is alive and well.

Using the very system it seeks to destroy, political correctness has stolen the desire for creative ingenuity. Individuality and those systems that hold Christian values are viewed as a threat to "change," and true American constitutionalists are nothing more than "radical crackpots." The effects of this political transformation are on the cutting edge of a tyrannical dictatorship.

In its fullest context the general principle of Jesus' role begins first by believing the consistencies in the story of His life and purpose rather than the eschatological discrepancies brought on by the likes of novice and professional Scriptural critics. By virtue of intent, the goal of Scriptural critics is not to inform as much as it is to influence the biblical inquirer to lean toward skepticism, which has brought us to this point of social demise in the first place. In the end times, however, choosing to partake in earthly ways is not covered under excuses for ignorance about the principalities for salvation. In order to be saved, one must believe that Jesus is God incarnate who reveals Himself to be the only saving grace from the tempest of political and social immoral reformation. When Jesus says, "I am the way and the truth and no man comes to the Father but by Me," this covers every aspect of the overall purpose for living. He is the way, the Redeemer, the Comforter, the Wayshower, and all things are and will be possible through Him. When the time is right, he will show all who He really is, and the ground on which all nations stand will be meaningless.

In terms of earthly deduction, the magnitude of Jesus' role in the up and coming events for this tumultuous world cannot be measured, let alone imagined. But what we do know for certain is the variety of love and hate for the man called Jesus. For example, despite the fact the continuity of the story line for the life and times of Jesus is consistent with the hundreds of millions who acknowledge the validity of His spiritual doctrines; Herbert H. Armstrong holds a contradictory but interesting position. In his book *Mystery of Ages*, Armstrong states, "The Church, founded by Jesus Christ, has an all-important meaning to every human life that ever lived. Yet almost no one has ever known the meaning. Even within the Christian world, apostasies, division, and changing times have blotted out the true original meaning and purpose that now is a mystery."[2] I say that Jesus will only be a mystery if you view Him as such. He is out there right before your eyes if you will accept Him into your heart. Also, what Jesus had come to do was reside in His church, and He is protected from those who seek to wipe clean His name from the face of the earth. This fact is admonished in Matthew 16:18 when Jesus said, "And I also say to you that thou art Peter, and upon this rock I will build my church, and the gates of Hell shall not prevail against it."[3]

Putting these words to the test, there are scholarly establishments and anti-Christian movements such as the Jesus Seminar that seek to make something of Jesus other than the essence of what He truly is. Whether or not they succeed will be determined by how the Christian world preserves the church and how far Christ will allow nonbelievers to go. Some of these anti-Christian groups go as far as to say that there never was a man called Jesus. The irony of these establishments is they consider their work as going unnoticed, but the likes of them is forewarned in the words of the very book they debase. 2 Timothy 4:3-4 alerts Christ's followers: "For the time will come when they will not endure sound doctrine, but according to their own desires, because they have itching ears, they will heap up for themselves teachers … and they will turn their ears away from the truth, and be turned aside to fables."[4] Because God reigns, the undisputable teachings of His truth will prevail no matter how much nonbelievers, scholarly or otherwise, try to discredit or refute the essence of His words. This especially applies to those individuals involved with the likes of anti-God movements.

It is "reasonable that intelligent believers should be aware of historical and critical issues"[5] that could potentially distort or impact Christian doctrines in the wrong way. This is why we must attend church, get involved in community, and never forget what we learn subjectively through Jesus as the object of our faith and not necessarily by the objective guidance of a minister or priest. The neophyte Christian will also find that studying the history of Jesus is entirely different from studying the theology of Jesus. Specifically, anti-Christian history often tries to explain the personal aspects of Jesus and His human life in a seductive but inaccurate way. No better example of this is from the scholarly endeavors of the Jesus Seminar. In as many ways as possible this group seeks to destroy every ounce of credibility acclaimed to Jesus including the refuting of His miracles down to the impossibility of His very existence. Therefore, when studying any works about the historical aspect of Jesus, a Christian should determine if critical work is done with good intention or even faithfully Christ-based at all. Secondly, it would be prudent to evaluate what the primary motives behind such an endeavor are because even if a work appears to be favorable, time spent on dissecting the words of Jesus suggests questionable faith about the teachings of Jesus and appears more like trying to disprove Him, categorically contributing to the deafening cadence of biblical defection.

This is why a Christian must never lose sight of being bound by faith in the theology of Jesus surrounding His divine life, death, and resurrection.

In support of my readiness to be critical, it would be advantageous to look to the scholarly wisdom of Albert Schweitzer. In his book _The Quest of the Historical Jesus_, Schweitzer states, "No man can justly criticize, or appraise the value of, new contributions to the study of this subject unless he knows in what forms they have been presented before."[6] I believe this study should include not only the works of the earliest Old Testament and New Testament church fathers, but works of Hermann Samuel Reimarus and anything in between on the way up to Robert Funk and his voluminous membership in the Jesus Seminar.

In the book _Revelation-Volume II_ by Vernon J. McGee, he states, "The gift of God is eternal life in Christ Jesus. And how do you get it? - But by faith. That is the only way you can receive a gift."[7] Therefore, if the work of the aforementioned anti-Christian establishments were with good intention, then the essence of faith alone would guide their work by the gift of the Holy Spirit. This is the persona that Jesus exudes in all there is.

The truth of the matter is, ever since Jesus' physical arrival on earth, the study of His life, ministry, and person has always been fair game for critical analysis. Even during the initial stages of following and listening to Jesus, His chosen disciples questioned who He really was and the scribes asked by what authority He performed His miracles. More than anything, and disregarding the fact that Jesus planned His death, what lead to Jesus' ultimate earthly demise was His open critical condemnation of the Sanhedrin who professed to be protecting the "pure" religious system handed down by Abraham and Moses. In addition, because of His Jewish heritage, Jesus' condemnation of the law keepers and His miracles were given even greater scrutiny. In the end, the survival of Jesus' teachings depended on meeting in secret, maintaining apostolic traditions, and preaching his infallible Word. But during the last two hundred years, the quest for the historical Jesus took on a formidable and identifiable form. It is here where the source and authentication of anti-Christian documents are dangerously hailed as indisputably accurate. But still there is no opposing force that can refute the fact that "All scripture is given by inspiration of God, and is profitable for doctrine, reproof, for correction, for instruction in righteous."[8] Scripture is the road map to salvation and God's grace.

Schweitzer says, "The authority for evaluating what these sources say belongs neither to the sources themselves nor to whoever wrote them. The authority belongs to the historian, the interpreter ... the historian may also consider the reasons for and motivations behind what happened."[9] This is partially why the historical process is so complex and dangerously wide open for scholarly critical intrusion into the words of a final historical document.

A clear example of this debate is seen in the words of Heinz Zahrnt. "History has become our fate. We must therefore pass everything which we think, and believe about Jesus through the sieve of strict methodological consideration, through the fire of historical criticism."[10] Zahrnt fails to mention that we have come to this point in history because we chose not to heed the words of Jesus Christ from the get-go. Had we done so, no doubt the world would be a better place. Instead, we question and look to "change" the very thing that works. Ironically, when we study the beginning of oral tradition, early written Biblical transcript and translation, the Apocrypha, the Torah, the Dead Sea Scrolls, the various implications of the Synoptic Gospels, and the sociopolitical movements of each of these specific times, we find they are all related and directly support the forthcoming life, death, and resurrection of Jesus Christ. But still, the bull's eye gets larger on the back of Christianity.

What would cause men to look beyond the initial literary context of the powerful words of Scripture? Is it fear, boredom, guilt, hatred of Jesus Christ and what He stands for, or is it the doings of the Evil One himself? These questions are but a few, but what we do know for certain is that critical analysis of the historical Jesus is alive and well and growing proportionately alongside the many applications of anti-Christian sentiment.

If I were asked when the quest of the historical Jesus first surfaced, I would say it began with the fearfully jealous ideations by the Pharisees, the Sadducees, and the blind obedient temple commoners who felt that Jesus was an imposter mocking the prophecy of the coming Messiah. Exhausting the rhetorical trickery of the Sanhedrin, we know that the religious authorities took Jesus to Pontius Pilate for no other reason than to ensure His condemnation and ultimate crucifixion. But because Jesus had his own plan so that we might live, He allowed His death to happen. Within this context, the connection between all circumstances leading to His, life, birth, and death gives us a better understanding of Jesus' role in the scheme of things.

Despite the Sanhedrin's hatred for Jesus, we still cannot brush aside the words of the gospel fact that "considered against this background, the earliest gospel tradition leads to Jesus who is recognizable as the just man, verified by his words and deeds, as a charismatic Jewish 'Holy Man'. This was the Jesus who lived [and died] under the rule of Pontius Pilate and as the contemporary of the Sanhedrin priestly hierarchy of the Temple."[11] These words cover both ends of the historical spectrum in that they constitute Jesus' earthly demise and are now reason for today's anti-Christian movements.

In terms of studying and evaluating the historical Jesus one of the most talked about early pioneers to take on this task was Samuel Reimarus. A professor of oriental languages in Hamburg, Germany, Reimarus worked to postulate an intense difference between who Jesus actually was and what His disciples proclaimed Him to be.

> Several of his writings appeared during his lifetime, all of them asserting the claims of rational religion as against the faith of the church; one of them was an essay on 'The Chief Truths of Natural religion.' His magnum opus, however, which laid the historic basis of his attacks, was circulating during his lifetime among his acquaintances, as an anonymous manuscript. Before Reimarus, no one had attempted to form a historical conception of the life of Jesus … The only interesting Life of Jesus written before Reimarus, was composed by a Jesuit in Persia. The author was the Indian missionary Hieronymus Xavier.[12]

Reimarus's most important work, *The Goal of Jesus and His Disciples*, was published in 1778 and "is generally accepted as the fragment which started the quest for the historical Jesus."[13] In relation to how God's kingdom works, the quest for the historical Jesus may have begun with Herod's quest to find the Messiah to kill Him. Although Herod's efforts failed, there is a new movement that seeks to kill Jesus through the distortion of words.

The significance of Reimarus's work lies in that "Reimarus made a distinction between the historical Jesus and the Jesus and the gospels. Much of the Gospel material, he claimed, as confessional and contradicted the historical facts, and thus hid the fact that Jesus was a political revolutionary."[14] This proclamation by itself, however, is nothing new. History shows that Jesus was considered a threatening political revolutionary even during His infamous trial. His open condemnation of the Sanhedrin is to that effect.

To his credit, it appears "Reimarus reconstructed the life of Jesus, more thoroughly than anyone had before; on thoroughly naturalistic assumptions.[15] This crucial point is supported by Schweitzer's portrayal of Reimarus. He suggests that Reimarus has no predecessors. Schweitzer also suggests that "before Reimarus, no one had attempted to form a historical conception of the life of Jesus."[16] Alluding to who Jesus is, we still have to ask what is it about Jesus that so many have put forth so much energy to destroy the image and character of a man who is the model for a vibrant hope?

Contrary to Schweitzer's description of Reimarus's singular importance, Raymond Martin states in his book *The Elusive Messiah* that Schweitzer's assessment of Reimarus is not accurate because "Reimarus, who was a child of the Enlightenment, was not before his time, but right on time. A host of thinkers-Spinoza, Pierre Bayle, the English Deists, and other-have paved the way for what Reimarus accomplished."[17]

Despite his gallant efforts, the endeavors of Reimarus still cannot escape the illuminating wisdom of Ecclesiastes 1:9: "The thing that hath been, it is that which shall be; and that which is done is that which shall be done: and there is no new thing under the sun."[18] These words in themselves point to Martin's contention for many great thinkers before Reimarus.

Although Reimarus had much to say about the historical Jesus, many of his concepts and observations were questionable. One of the most absurd is his hypothesis about Jesus' death and resurrection. Reimarus felt that Jesus cried, "My God, My God, why have you forsaken Me," only because He did not intend to suffer and die but to build a worldly kingdom and deliver the Israelites from bondage. Reimarus overlooks the fact that Jesus could have saved Himself. Concerning Jesus' death, Reimarus also said the reason the disciples undertook their deception and fabrication of the stolen body of Jesus was their desire to avoid turning to their mundane ways of making a living in Galilee."[19] Although it has happened before, it is difficult to conceive that someone would take such a marvelous piece of history and try to get into the minds of men to postulate motivation without an opportunity to defend themselves.

Similarly, in all fairness to Reimarus, unless we know exactly what was going through his mind at the time of his work, we can only presuppose what his intentions were. Obviously, because he was apprehensive about releasing his work publicly with his name on it, he may not have fully believed what he was writing. But at the same time, there is no getting away from what appears to be Reimarus's initial intent. He approached his work with the sole purpose of clarifying an absolute distinction between apostolic writings and what Jesus Himself proclaimed and taught in His own lifetime. I have to say that although Reimarus would not admit it, he discovered that there are no words by any man that can separate the truths of what the gospel writers had written about the teachings of Jesus because the teachings themselves are the reason for the gospel.

While not impossible, it still remains truly difficult to itemize all the specific procuring causes for the interest and rise of men such as Reimarus. For such an answer I believe the church can look to itself. Specifically, "once the four gospels were established as scripture within the early Church, they were interpreted to support faith and doctrine. [But] no distinction was made between the Christ of faith and the Jesus history [because] strictly speaking, there was no problem and no quest for the historical Jesus."[20] But because the church leaders and opponents of Christianity were well aware of the obvious differences in the gospels, something had to be done to protect the sanctity of Christian doctrine and its history. Subsequently, "over the centuries, many numbers of attempts were made to harmonize and to defend the apparent discrepancies in the Gospel account."[21] Despite good intention by dedicated Christian proponents, efforts at corrective measures have left the door wide-open for negative outside forces to come in and establish an entirely different slant on the concept of Christianity and the man called Jesus. Thus, the saga of identifying and solidifying the role of Jesus in the overall scheme of things continues.

Although not all encompassing, W. Barnes Tatum suggests a plausible hypothesis, which may have contributed to the rise of the quest for the historical Jesus. Tatum asserts that "the enlightenment [period], not the Reformation, provided the intellectual setting for rigorous historical research in, through, and behind the four Gospels for Jesus. The emergence of the quest of the historical Jesus occurred virtually simultaneously with renewed interest on the literary relationship among the four Gospels. Now both the Gospels and Jesus are often considered without regard for the traditional ways that had been viewed within the Church."[22] Does this search mean that man doubts his own capacity for goodness?

Albert Schweitzer has a different perspective on the quest to know the historical Jesus. His hypothesis resolves around the emotions of men rather than clarification and specificities of documents. He states,

> No vital force comes into the figure unless a man breathes into it all the hate or all the love of which he is capable. The stronger the love, or the stronger the hate, the more lifelike is the figure which is produced. For hate as well as love can write a Life-Of-Jesus and the greatest of them are written with hate are those of Reimarus, the Wolfenbuttle Fragmentist, and that of David Friedrich Strauss.

> It was hate not so much of the person Jesus as of the supernatural nimbus with which it was so easy to surround him, and with which he had in fact been surrounded. They were eager to picture him as an ordinary person, to strop from him the robes of splendor with which he had been appareled, and clothe him once more with the coarse garments in which he had walked in Galilee. And their hate sharpened their historical insight.[23]

However enlightening Schweitzer's statement might be, it is not a foregone conclusion that Schweitzer's proclamation is drawn solely from the works of previous Biblical scholars. All he had to do was observe how Christians treated one another.

Judging from the intensity of critical analysis on the subject matter, in all due respect, the endeavors of men like Reimarus have truly taken

Scriptural context to a level of microscopic absurdity bordering on the ridiculous. Following this line of thinking, what makes a stove hot has little to do with why not to touch it.

Taking a hard look at the egotism of historical critical assessment of Jesus' life, the topic of debate discussed in *The Social Setting of Jesus and the Gospels* by Wolfgang, Stegman, Malina, and Theissen is rather interesting. The argument brought forth is what is determined to be a general consensus among New Testament scholars concerning the baptism of Jesus. "Most New Testament scholars engaged in Gospel and historical Jesus research conclude that Jesus of Nazareth underwent baptism at the hand of John the Baptizer, but they found nothing historically reliable in the events immediately following the baptism - Mark 1:9 -11; cf. Matthew 3:13 -17; and Luke 3:21-22. Many place what is reported after Jesus' baptism, explicitly or implicitly, in the category of legend (Bultmann 1963:247) or myth (Dibelius 1934:271)."[24] Issues such as these are what makes eschatological inquiry appear ridiculously ineffective.

In reality, does it make a difference that we know what Jesus did after His baptism? Would it make a difference or be possible to know exactly what Jesus did from the time He was born until the time that He died? Is it possible that after all the written transcriptions from the oral tradition and translations into various languages, scrutiny by religious communities and counsels, and input by both learned and unlearned men that somewhere, somehow, copyists made an error in judgment or decided personal preferential treatment of a document is better than what is stated? Although these arguments seem plausible, we must never forget who wrote, who transcribed, and under what religious and sociopolitical conditions Scripture came into being: "All scripture is given by inspiration of God, and is profitable for doctrine, for reproof, for correction, for instruction, in righteous."[25] The inspirational Biblical gift from God has turned into a senseless and catastrophic argument, and at the same time, the conscripts of Scripture and the freedoms of America allow for this absurdity to continue.

On the other hand, a strong proponent for clarifying the validity of Jesus and scriptural content is G.A. Wells. In his book *The Historical Evidence for Jesus*, he presents his work in such a way that he avoids including anything that atheists have written on Christianity. But he also dances softly around his conclusions and states, "I do not of course claim to have proven my views correct. If the evidence were such that in theory could be established to the exclusion of all others, the whole question [of the quest of the historical Jesus] would have been settled long ago."[26]

Another strong proponent of the validity of Jesus was Martin Kahler. He was an activist against the liberal theology that slowly conquered most of the theological chairs at German universities. At the time, this was a critical and bold move because the majority of the quest for the historical Jesus proponents came from German theological scholarly perspectives. Kahler was unique in that he "was aware of the problems by the developments in philosophy and by the historical research into biblical literature. He was also a strictly systematic thinker who developed his ideas under the principle of the Reformers-justification by 'grace'- without repeating the traditional formulations of Protestant Orthodoxy."[27]

In reference to the problems of the historicity of Jesus Christ, in his book *Where is History Going?* John Warwick Montgomery says, "Whence arises content? Evidently not from the character of the historical evidence for Jesus' life, since the documentary testimonies relating to Him are not qualitatively different from the evidence upon which testimonies relating to Him are not qualitatively different from the evidence upon which portraits of other historical figures are built."[28] What makes Jesus' history more of a target is that His teachings and sacrifice hold people accountable and responsible for what they do. Unlike a politician who looks to making decisions based on the survival of his own political future, Jesus made all his decisions knowing that His decisions would ultimately lead to the demise of His physical life so that we may live. His Medal of Honor is long overdue.

Having looked at the upsurge in biblical analysis, there are four distinct time periods that are generally accepted as definitive eras relative to the quest for the historical Jesus. "The Old Quest, 1778-1906; an interim period or 'No Quest,' from 1906 to 1953; the New Quest, from 1953 to the present day; and the Third Quest, from the early 1980's until the present day."[29] The early inception of the quest of the historical Jesus movement has allowed it to maintain a dramatic influence, while not all positive, on the Christology and historicity of Jesus Christ and the Christian movement; the most recent is the Jesus Seminar. The irony is that while good people focus on fighting the opponents of Jesus, society falls deeper into the quagmire of self-destruction.

What is the Jesus Seminar? Founded by Robert Funk, the Jesus Seminar purports their goals are to determine who Jesus really was and to free the church of centuries-old improper interpretation of Jesus' work and words. They also argue against the accurate historicity of the New Testament documents. Without getting into the actual methodology and presuppositions of their work, there is no current scholarly consensus about the significance of their conclusions. Still, the effort of their work is polluting long-held traditions concerning the sanctity of the man called Jesus. Their conclusion is that Jesus was nothing more than a very wise man with a distinct character and personality but not in any miraculous or apocalyptic way as believers portray Him to be.

How does this movement relate to the original scholastic efforts of anti-Christian history? In order to prove their stand, the Jesus Seminar has simply used questionable items of Scripture, which may seem inconclusive, contradictory, unlikely, and questionable. This includes Jesus' miracles, death and resurrection, and the promise of His return. From this base they then use this criterion to move to disprove the validity of Christ. Irrefutably, they have an extremely liberal and unwarranted approach to interpreting origin, purpose, and ideology of the Christian movement with the sole purpose to rewrite and destroy what the man Jesus Christ had come to fulfill.

Perhaps it would be wise for scholars to heed the words of Martin Kahler. Kahler cautions that "the Life-Of-Jesus movement is a blind alley … but is completely in the right insofar as it sets the bible against an abstract dogmatism. It becomes illegitimate as soon as it begins to rend and dissect the bible without having acquired a clear understanding of the special nature of the problem and the peculiar significance of Scripture for such understanding."[30] Clearly, more time should be spent on appreciating and practicing the teachings of Jesus rather than loathing over the validity of His message.

Although carrying a great deal of scholarly weight, Kahler's aforementioned warning continues to be unimportant and blatantly denied by the likes of agnostic movements, various scholarly circles, and anti-Christian establishments. They would much rather spend their efforts discrediting the church of Jesus, and, in some instances, hoping to disprove there ever was a man called Jesus Christ. But as history has demonstrated, they have not been able to erase the impact of truths derived from Scriptural authority. More importantly, there is a clear distinction between those who do not believe Jesus' message and those who do. When the nonbelievers dig deeper they find that the building blocks of Christianity and its ardent principles live on and continue to gain ever more strength through what is promised in Malachi 3:1: "Behold, I will send my messenger and he shall prepare the way before me; and the Lord whom ye speak, shall suddenly come to his temple even the messenger of the covenant, whom ye delight in, he shall come, saith the Lord of hosts."[31]

Stirring the pot we discover not everything about the quest for disproving the historical Jesus is negative. In fact, there is much to be learned from the criticism of such anti-Christian scholarly movements. For one, because its greatest ally is to dissect words, phrases, and contextual inferences of given passages, this process helps the student of Scripture to be more proactive in their studies and to rely more on what they have been taught and to see what has worked. This opens the door for proof of what God's Word accomplishes and what it stands for. More importantly, the works of the refuting scholars help to increase faith, encouraging recognition of God's principles in a hands-on practical form. This is where the refuting scholars have failed to add substance to their hypotheses. They cannot explain the end result of what faith can do and why it works.

Merely reading the Bible does not ensure understanding of its contents because sound biblical study is a lifetime endeavor and could easily become an all-inclusive one. But when an individual actually pursues serious comparisons between anti-Jesus movements with gospel proclamations, they will discover that negative assumptions and presumptions about Scripture cannot compete with the truths of the gospel because Scripture is a living document that speaks for itself. Prophecies are fulfilled and man's self-destructive ways away from Scripture are slowly leading him to his ultimate demise.

Perhaps Martin Luther had the best earthly analogy when he stated, "The gospels follow no order in recording the acts and miracles of Jesus, and the matter is, after all, of much importance. If a difference arises in regard to Holy Scripture and we cannot solve it, we must let it alone."[32] The point being, it is bad policy to disturb the graves of our ancestors. Some things are meant to be left to themselves.

In conclusion, when one studies the magnitude of what Scripture purports, it is unlikely that an answer or rebuttal to address any circumstance encompassing the vicissitudes of life could not be found. From cover to cover, it is the defender of the beginning and the end of times as well as a psychological text designed to cure all doubt as to who we are and what purpose we might serve. Given this proposition, one could only speculate about the level of surprise, confusion, and elation that the Jesus Seminar movement would experience if they met the same fate as did Paul on his way to Damascus. Of certainty, mankind will come to realize that taking Christ out of the scheme of things is the biggest mistake he has ever made.

Above and beyond all rhetoric, proclamations, and scholarly endeavors, nothing says it better than 2 Timothy 1:13: "Hold fast the form of sound words, which thou hast heard of me, in faith and love which is in Christ Jesus."[33]

V

WHAT IS THE FUTURE FOR A BIBLICAL
SOCIAL CONSCIENCE?

Before responding to the question what is the future for Biblical social conscience, I must first return to the prescription I proposed earlier: in order to fully understand and grasp the principles of God's law, one must first believe that there is a God and that Scripture is the Word of God. Otherwise the richest concepts for the following discussion would be completely embedded in baseline constructs away from those of intent. Working from this theological premise we can then move to open dialogue for some reasons as to why the world increasingly is blindly following the drowning ways of self-destruction.

We can begin by first saying abandoning the Christian God is fast becoming "in vogue" and more of a special problem than some care to admit. Some of this is due to the disparities between creation and science, but a large portion is attributed to the demise of family structure and shifting social value systems. Indubitably, the "free love" concept of the 1960s left its indelible mark on the social structure of America; especially in the area of parents neglecting to teach their children the traditional fundamentals of a creation God. Reaching maturity, the end result is the development of more and more "freethinkers" that abandon traditional religion and look for, as some "celebrities" suggest, other spiritual avenues to heaven. The side effects of this disemboweling defection are seen in looseness of integrity, morals, ethics, and experimentation in most every sphere of human life. This looseness is not necessarily limited to the general population. There has been a dramatic increase of all sorts of immoral improprieties in political circles and some religious circles as well. The danger of this shift is that, as John Warwick Montgomery put it, "If the biblical foundations of Law and Gospel are neglected, or relegated to a position of secondary importance, all will be lost, including our freedoms and any possibility of genuine progress: vacuum coffins will indeed become the order of the day."[1] One of the routes these events culminate is best described by Saint Theophan the Recluse. He said, "The instrument by which the demons express their will power in this world is the whole aggregate of worldly customs, which are impregnated with and steeped in sinful elements. These worldly customs stupefy a man and seduce him from God."[2] Satan is alive and well.

What Montgomery and Saint Theophan are suggesting is that sinful ways can only continue to replicate if man willfully removes himself from the premise that God is the undisputed center for distinguishable well-being. God clearly wants this for us, otherwise He never would have said, "Be ye therefore perfect, even as your Father which is in heaven is perfect."[3] What better argument is there that these statements not be construed merely as philosophical fiction but having a distinct and important place in the overall scheme of things? Thus, this chapter will show how the relevancy of conscience centered in God typifies a sense of worth and purpose when attempting to fulfill the passions of the heart.

For a number of reasons, the nature of conscience relative to Christian doctrine has always been of special interest to me, and I would hate to think what kind of society we would have without it. But at the same time, "many people have never studied moral theology but are exemplary Christians who lead virtuous lives and make good moral decisions. So the model goes one does not have to study moral theology to be a good Christian."[4] The answer to this question is obviously no. But we must also keep in mind that whether or not an individual believes in God, moral reasoning does not come from evolution. Moral reasoning comes from various stages of human development which is influenced by education, guidance, social interaction, and belief systems that ultimately contribute to the creative development of a particular mindset. Having considered the aforementioned premise, knowing that a client may be guilty, lawyers by definition try to defend the actions of their client by looking for ways around the law. So in principle, what does this say about the conscience and integrity of a lawyer that happens to be a Christian? What Stuart Hampshire says about such a question makes sense. "This resemblance between the practical reasoning of lawyers about the law and practical reasoning on matters of moral concern is imperfect."[5] Imperfection then, transpires because of conflict in the application of principles. So how does one maintain principles without offending moral reasoning? I believe Lewis B. Smeade says it best: "Truthfulness of being is an ideal we struggle toward. It is hard for us to be whole inside and out because we are complicated and confused within."[6] Following Smeade's model, the exercising of moral obligation is difficult because there are many variables leading up to the choice between good and evil.

In today's world there are so many different complications of power that add to the struggle for maintaining consistency in our thinking that it makes choosing between good and evil very difficult. For example, if confronted by an identical situation in two different incidences, by what criteria will one make a choice to satisfy the needs of one individual over another when both are struggling to the same affect? Will that choice be predicated on consistency or do we justify personal motivation for supporting our choice? In answer to this question we might look to Hampshire's quote of Aristotle's moral theory, which says, "Moral injunctions are to be thought of as a protection against a warped character, monstrous ambitions, corrupt appetites, and stunted and inhuman sentiments."[7] Not that this makes decision making any easier, but in many ways Aristotle's words help to diminish the condemnation of most anyone who goes astray. Before anything, we must keep in mind that we are all humans first. But this is not to say that we should not be held accountable and responsible for the decisions we make. Though this may be true in principle, but unfortunately we live in a duplicitous society, and much of what men say and do sometimes escapes the truthful scrutiny from others. When there is enough money to provide for the best council most anyone can get away with murder.

While there are endless philosophical and theological discussions on ethics and morals, they all seem to be governed by the logic that "an agent who acts for a reason is moved to act by his or her representations of the world as it is and as it might be."[8] But if we live by this model we must agree there is no such thing as a permanent pattern. There is always the exception to the rule. Case in point, judging from the ongoing defection from biblical moral and ethical constraints, man's legacy as a higher animal is having difficulty in maintaining civility to that acclaim. Foremost, out of the mist of this changing human condition are two enduring questions. How can we measure decent progressive morals and ethics from a backsliding conscience, and what will be the subsequent glue that holds together everything a man ordains? Assuredly, without Christianity we would have a completely discombobulated society. But as we have seen, the courts and government are now in the business of legislating immorality.

Not that a Christian conscience will always ensure gravitation toward goodness each and every time, but an aware Christian conscience does help to sort out and categorize justifications for detouring from or gravitating to the obligations of leading a conscionable life. This, in conjunction with reason, determines success or failure and ultimately portrays what kind of world we will live in.

B. Gert has an interesting take on the aforementioned ideas. He argues that "evil plays a much more important role in morality than good does."[9] Should Gert be correct, whatever happened to the normative claim that man is separated from other animals by his higher executive functioning giving him the ability to unravel and discern the complexities of deductions and configurations induced by thought? A more important question to consider is why is the surrender to the world of stimulation so easy when dealing with the vicissitudes of life? The answer to this question can only be found in the rejection or partaking in a certain way of life determined by choices away from God. Satan is alive and well.

Equipped with such a complex mechanism as conscience, what controlling factor would cultivate a pledge for righteous certainties? A reasonable schematic application is obvious: either man takes on the belief that there is a divine principle at work and he needs to follow that path, or he will simply live and die by the choices he makes.

There can be little disagreement that my contention throughout has been reason and conscience at the time of the fall as the turning point from bliss to the sometimes unconscionable lawlessness of man. But even so, from where and at what point in time did Eve acquire the desire to even think in terms defecting if she did not already have the knowledge of reason or the awareness of a conscience to know the difference? If we were to consider Gilbert Ryle's take on conscience we would have to say that Eve was at a point where her commonsense conscience was her worst enemy. Ryle believes that a person's conscience is "provoked only by his own actions or thoughts and not by others."[10] Undoubtedly tied to this principle are personal accountability and responsibility, something we tend to forget. Using Ryle's principle, we would have to say that Eve was not enticed by Satan and that she was responsible for her own choice. But even if Eve was personally mentally responsible for what she was about to experience, we still cannot disregard the possibility of satanic influence, especially since we have yet to discern if her action was or was not consciously and willfully induced.

In trying to validate the existence and impact of conscience, is it possible that God gave Eve a conscience as a test for allegiance? But then again too, why would God test Eve if she was already pure in thought and had the capacity to understand the difference between good and evil? Or did she? Either way, one would think because of her assumed pureness Eve had a superior capacity for achieving better results. To each of these questions we must return to the premise of having an appreciation for God in His simplest form before we can consider the layers of universal relevancy tied to His greatness. But I still have to ask: if God demands our undivided attention, why did He increase our autonomy through freedom of choice?

Garth L. Hallett seems to think that the Christian faces this dichotomy every day. He says, "For what we want to know is how a Christian should choose between alternative, incompatible actions, which he will then deliberately discontinue or deliberately undertake."[11] I would have to say that the only answer to this formidable statement is conscience is the sounding board and driving force behind the motivation for everything we do.

Russell Hardin takes a different approach to the causal relations between good as well as bad choices. He thinks, "If I take the time to calculate the consequences of various courses of action before me, then I will ipso facto have chosen the course of action to take, namely, to sit and calculate, because while I am calculating the other sources of action will cease to be open to me."[12] As evidenced by the end result, apparently Eve did not calculate her choices or the consequences. Adding to the seemingly unbalanced emphasis of the garden story, we have to think as to why Eve even made the choice that she did because at the beginning there was very little social interaction that could have induced such a choice based on experience. This leaves the door wide open for three, but not all-inclusive, scenarios: one, the garden incident was designed to fail; two, Eve was influenced by an outside element; or three, Eve's decision was definitely a conscionable act.

Moving away from deliberating the nature and origin of conscience, we can now turn to various absolutes that realistically itemize man's culpability for choices contrary to the laws of God.

Because of man's need to know, new intellectual frontiers have opened the door to announcing, explaining, postulating, and justifying why man does what he does. Of course, this premise is not all-inclusive because sometimes there is no explanation for what triggers a person to deviate from a customary norm as people know it to be. I support this viewpoint because due to the unpredictability of man, he will not always respond to the same set of circumstances every time in the same way. Thus, the best way to protect against the unexplainable is to always expect the unexpected from the fallibilities of an uncomplimentary, unconscionable conscience away from reason. This is especially true since motivation is not always visibly discernible.

Given the known academic explanations for a person's role in the confines of environment, social law, psychological descriptors, and independent action, these have become the criteria that contribute to the development, understanding, and labeling of a person as a whole. Then the whole is sent into the world represented by personal character that has been formed by influence, reason, and motivation. The strength of reason is then tested by conscience, which completes the groundwork for or against a better life. Before it is too late, there is no better way to tie all this together than by having a belief and faith in Christ because we all have a date with destiny and will be judged accordingly. It will be at this time He will say, "Now is the end come upon thee, and I will send mine anger upon thee, and will judge thee according to thy ways, and will recompense upon thee all thine abominations."[13]

There are many significant contributing factors that are evidenced with the aforementioned formula, but none is more important than a genuine and sincere commitment to Christ. This precept is supported and held together by an abundance of indisputable spiritual evidence cited in Scripture. Some examples can be found in Romans 1:11, 15:27, 1 Corinthians 10:3, 15:44, and Ephesians 1:3, 5:19.[14]

Not so surprisingly, although these truths are revered by millions of followers, historically they have been undermined not only by non-Christians but by those fallen Christians who partake in the same self-indulgences, lack of social respect, and immoral acts normally attributed to heathens. Caught between knowing what is right but doing what is wrong in many ways is double jeopardy, making the essence of choice paramount to the equation. But, for the many unbelievers who willfully indulge in such behavioral turbulence, knowledge or concern for moral and spiritual choices that have eternal consequences may not be part of the educational tutorial for a better life. In other words, the thought of salvation and regenerating the soul through something that cannot be seen physically could not possibly satisfy the gratifications derived from self-indulgence. As there is nothing new under the sun, this irresponsible and negligent behavioral mindset is reproved in Job 8:13. "So are the paths of all those that forget God and the hypocrite's hope shall perish."[15] Additional condemnation of self-indulgence is also seen in John 6:63. "It is the spirit that quickeneth; the flesh profiteth nothing: the words that I speak unto you, they are spirit, and they are life."[16]

Whether drugs, alcohol, pornography, or infidelity are single-handedly or collectively responsible for an individual's fall, in terms of change, it takes a great deal of effort to override any entrenched or crystallized desire for self-indulgence. This problem is further exacerbated if the individual relates to aversive habits as a comfort zone and does not truly want to change. Complicating matters, it is even more difficult to try to replace a negative indulgence with something like the redeeming theological qualities found in Scripture or any type of representation for a spiritual consociation. These are intangible items and have little to do with the world of self-indulgence. This is especially true when asked to worship something unseen that is purported to be greater than you. This type of spiritual deficit is defined in Matthew 6:21. "For where your treasure is, there will be your heart also."[17]

In America and throughout the world, the self-indulgent mindset of social immorality and unethical practices is clearly on the rise and is exemplified through various aspects of media, education and government officials, and self-proclaimed avatars. The unfortunate aspect of this travesty is that most any age group can be subjected to these immoral threats. Resulting mental strain and peripheral devastation created by such perversity translates to an economic and moral burden for society overall. There is an ongoing process of lifelong conflict and challenge for the individual abuser.

Given the liberal "new age" way of thinking, self-indulgence in family circles is partially brought on by parents who, by virtue of their own immorality cause their children to search for love and affection from other adverse sources. Filling this gap are adverse media such as negative and violent television, violent motion pictures, immoral theatrical plays, the world of macabre, and video games with horrific content and influence. How this translates to the real world is the total breakdown of respect for teachers, fraudulent use of social institutions, disregard for long-held social traditions, no interest in responsibility, and a tremendous sense of entitlement. In clinical terms, these are the classic personality characteristics of an Antisocial Personality Disorder. Thus, looking to parental inattentiveness and lack of guidance is not simply a case for projection of blame. But it is safe to say that neglectful parents greatly contribute to the godless children of the current generation and the negative residual that follows. Without a God foundation, what we are left with is a personality riddled with insensitivity and apathy, which was never intended to be part of man's psychological makeup. But ever since the fall and the intentional elimination of God, social conscience has found more comfort in showing reverence for Hollywood idolatry and political figures than for God. Some might say that if we were to examine Old Testament Biblical history we would see many of the same abominations and obscenities, so what's the big deal? The deal is we would also see that God became angry and intervened.

If someone were to ask me where I thought social conscience was headed, I'd have to earnestly say because the path to Christ is attacked more and more each day, the negative aspects of conscience have exceeded the tip of the wedge and worsened. In support of the preceding statement I will offer some ideas as to why I am not very optimistic about the future of social conscience. I chose these particular early examples of biblical defection largely because they are examples of what was to come.

Conscience in Euthanasia

In many ways, conscience is generally limited to having to choose between two variables. To achieve a desired result, also included is what appears to be a choice between a right way and a wrong way. But out of these constraints there is also an element of conscience that has to deal with certain prejudices that might be critical to justifying moral elements when arguing for or against certain preferences. Such is evidenced in cases concerning the morality of euthanasia and artificial insemination. Although I do not have a specific stance on either of these topics I chose these two particular issues for discussion because they are the pinnacle of showing how far man is willing to go once he leaves behind the good conscience associated with a creation God.

The issue of euthanasia is not new to society, nor has it been an issue only relative to the free thinkers of the 1960s. According to Margaret Jasper, "The Greeks saw sickness as a curse and actually endorsed suicide … suicide was seen as worthy, noble, and humane choice."[18] "Over time, the voluntary act of suicide ultimately developed into an organized voluntary euthanasia process lead by advocates such as the Hemlock Society, Compassion in Dying, Euthanasia Research and Guidance Organization, and the late Dr. Jack Kevorkian, who assisted his first known suicide patient in 1990."[19]

Practitioners of euthanasia had free rein until the church became involved around the second and third centuries. "Christianity took hold and suicide was denounced … The rationale was that death could only be determined by God, and that human suffering was divinely ordained and to be borne no matter how great the affliction."[20] Later on, the "Catholic and Protestant hierarchy adhered to the position that mercy killing was a violation of God's sixth commandment prohibiting murder, and ran against God's divine will."[21]Although there are some countries that still practice mercy killing, religious movements and the courts in America remain steadfast in their efforts to eradicate the practice of legal and illegal euthanasia.

Despite early civilization's acceptance and practice of euthanasia, "The voluntary euthanasia movement in the United States began during the first part of the twentieth century. It consisted primarily of scholarly, even esoteric debate that had little impact on public policy."[22] However, it was also "during this time, a number of mercy killings were undertaken in Europe and America. The legal consequences varied greatly. There were harsh murder convictions in some cases, and acquittals in numerous other cases."[23]

Over time, the subject of euthanasia has developed into a strongly debated argument incorporating the scrutiny of the medical profession, various religious groups, state legislatures, and court systems at both the state and federal level.

Although aggressive, organized activist movements have gained leaps and bounds in favor of euthanasia, right-to-life movements also have gained strength by utilizing the argument of medical technical and mechanical aspects, which have been designed for sustaining life. Some approaches to high-tech medicine include cardiac pulmonary resuscitation (CPR), feeding tubes, respirators, antibiotics, and life support systems that essentially operate all of one's necessary bodily functions. However proficient these procedures may be, the real problem begins when the court, medical arena, and advocacy groups debate over whose life should end. Advanced medical achievements may be instrumental in creating and prolonging life, but who makes the decision to take life? Who has the ethical right to take life and at what point should the decision be made?

The argument for the decisive moment to take life can be found in the President's Commission Report.

> Within less than a decade of the publication of the President's Commission Report, another contentious issue was put to rest by the United State Supreme Court, at least for legal purposes, that is, whether it was legally permissible to withhold or withdraw artificial nutrition and hydration. Reflecting the officially promulgated positions of several clinical professional organizations, the court adopted the position that artificial nutrition and hydration was a medical treatment and that for purposes of making decisions about its withholding or withdrawal, it should be treated the same as any other medical treatment. Thus, withholding a feeding tube from a terminally ill patient pursuant to the decision of one who had the authority to make such a decision should not be thought of as starving a patient and thus is not legally culpable.[24]

This legal proclamation is rather explicit in its presentation and is morally and legally problematic for those groups who oppose the practice of medically-assisted euthanasia.

About thirty years ago, James Rachel brought to bear another controversial aspect when he wrote one of the most well-known papers on the semantics of medical ethics of euthanasia. Rachel states, "The distinction between active and passive euthanasia is thought to be crucial for medical ethics. The idea is that permissible, at least in some cases, to withhold treatment and allow a patient to die, but it never permissible to take any direction designed to kill the patient."[25]

Rachael's idea of passive and active euthanasia, however, has been attacked from a variety of authoritative sources. For example, "The House of Lords Select Committee on Medical Ethics describes 'the term passive euthanasia' as 'misleading' and the British Medical Association calls the expression 'active' and 'passive' euthanasia ambiguous and unhelpful claiming that confusion may ... arise when the withdrawing or withholding of life-prolonging treatment which is not providing a benefit to the patient is described as euthanasia."[26]

While both sides of the euthanasia issue continue to profess and debate over each other's position, in the 2005 article "Ethics and Law: Physician-Assisted Dying, Dr. Meisel, MD, attempts to bring both sides of the argument closer together by stating, "Although sometimes ethical precepts, legal prescriptions, and clinical practices diverge, there is a tremendous amount of similarity among them."[27] Dr. Meisel bases his opinion on the fact that similarities "stem from the iterative and dialectical manner on which the consensus has developed, involving not only law-making and ethical analysis but also clinical practice and governmental and professional policy making."[28]

The cause of such diverse and controversial opinion is a topic unto itself, but the real question, however, lies not in the practical application of a particular opinion or platform concerning life and death. The real question lies somewhere between motivational factors and the root cause of a particular belief system. Is it merely on the pretext that the First Amendment of the United States Constitution guarantees every individual the right to freedom of expression or is it simply because critical thinking has become more flexible and sensitive to accommodate popular viewpoints and political pressure? What about the inclusion and exclusion of religious beliefs concerning euthanasia? Waldo Beach says, "At funeral services, Christians are assured of the victory over death in the blessed life to come. However, our general cultural context has become so secularized that the prevailing axiom is that this life is all there is."[29] For whatever reason, social mores, values, and legalities continue to be challenged by the diverse appetites of social demand involving their relationship between doctors, patients, and the state.

Over the years, both sides of the argument of euthanasia have won and lost strength in their position. John Mills attempted to simplify and shed new light on this argument by stating, "The only way in which a human being can make some approach to knowing the whole of a subject is by hearing what can be said about it by persons of every variety of opinion and studying all modes in which it can be looked at by every character of mind. No wise man ever acquitted his wisdom in any mode by this."[30] Given this approach to discussion, it is not intellectually difficult to accept the "Carter-Reagan Presidential bioethics commission's report, which ultimately transformed the ethical consensus into a legal one."[31]

One of the most controversial legal battles concerning the ethics of euthanasia is the Terri Schiavo case. "Since her collapse in 1990, Mrs. Schiavo had been assumed to be in a 'persistent vegetative state', legally defined in a Florida statute as a 'permanent and irreversible condition of unconsciousness' from which no recovery is possible. Withdrawal of nutrition and hydration permitting 'natural death' was therefore appropriate in a 'terminal condition' like Mrs. Schiavo's where end-of-life protocols are legally permitted in Florida statutes for end-state cases."[32] This is a prime example of suffering the fate handed down by the judicial and medical system.

Although the medical field ultimately made the final decision about Schiavo's prognosis for long-term quality of life and the ultimate discontinuation of her life, no one really knows for certain what the medical outcome for Schiavo would have been had she been allowed to remain on her support system. Of certainty, "the story of the public debate surrounding Terri Schiavo should impress laypersons and professionals alike the uncertainty of the context in which issues of continuation and termination are argued ethically."[33]

Debated for many years, it was determined that Schiavo could no longer return to the sanctity of life; therefore, she should be removed from the life-sustaining apparatus. Subsequently, she died from starvation and dehydration. Was this immoral in itself? The ethical framework and final decision on which this case was argued has certainly influenced the outcome of present judicial, medical, and ethical decisions.

Despite the high-profile status of the Schiavo case, there have also been previous cases that were instrumental in bringing euthanasia to the forefront of debate. Specifically, "end-of-life decision making became a matter of public discourse in the mid-1970's with the commencement of litigation in the Karen Ann Quinlan case ... it was probably the mix of new life sustaining technologies and the medical malpractice crisis of the 1970's, plus some intangible factors of the personalities involved that propelled the Quinlan case from clinic to court."[34] Consequently, cases involving conflicts about end-of-life decision making have become a staple of medical practice, bioethics discourse, and judicial and legislative lawmaking ever since. It doesn't stop here. Because of a high vulnerability index for malpractice suits, there is a mass exodus from the field of obstetrics.

Who has not heard of the infamous Dr. Kevorkian? Dr. Kevorkian's approach to euthanasia gained much attention because he stood fast in his belief about medically-assisted euthanasia and defied the requests of courts to cease his assisted suicide activity. His defiance brought euthanasia out of the closet and onto the television screen. Kevorkian's physician-assisted euthanasia was only applied where it was apparent that the prognosis for recovery was bleak. The problem with this analysis is that there have been many, many incidences where prayer groups have turned around what appeared to be the end for a patient. In such cases doctors cannot or will not commit to an explanation. Ultimately, Kevorkian's defiance of the courts led to his incarceration for second-degree murder in March 1999. Without Kevorkian's efforts, however, it is certain many of the unanswered and debated questions concerning medically-assisted suicide would have been delayed. He had become the sacrificial lamb so to speak.

According to Margaret Jasper, "Polls show that a growing number of Americans support honoring a patient's request for voluntary active euthanasia."[35] However, contrary to this public support is the argument that "respirators and food delivery systems could now keep a terminally ill or comatose patient breathing and nourished, even, if that meant living their life hooked up to some type of machinery for an unknowable period of time."[36] This is why a last will and testament is important.

In a much-publicized case, the movement against euthanasia acquired a boost in their pro-life position in February 2005. On August 4, 2005, the CBS 5:00 evening news reported that Farrah Scanlon, who was struck by a drunk driver and left in a comma for over twenty years, had miraculously awakened. Not only did she awaken, it was reported that she was cognizant of the events around the terrorist attacks on September 11 and the Oklahoma City bombing. This in itself is a mystery. Had this individual been subjected to medically-assisted euthanasia, the end result would certainly be different. This case certainly brings new light to the extremely emotional public battle concerning the fate of Terri Schiavo. We will never know what might have been had she not been relieved of her life supports.

Whether inside or outside the perimeters of the legal arena, one of the most prevailing problems concerning the issue of euthanasia is that of general consensus concerning the issue of standard interpretation and categorization of terminologies, viewpoints, and legalities of each particular state. Until a uniform code of law is constructed to govern euthanasia, this matter will certainly be one of debate for years to come.

Taken from the book *Koop-The memories of America's Family Doctor* by C. Everett Koop, MD, the ethics issue of euthanasia could not have been summed up better. Koop states,

> We must be wary of those who are too willing to end lives of the elderly and the ill. If we ever decide that a poor quality of life justifies ending a life, we have taken a step down a slippery slope that places all of us in danger. There is a difference between allowing nature to take its course and actively assisting death. The call for euthanasia surfaces in our society periodically, as it is doing now under the guise of 'death dignity' or assisted suicide. Euthanasia is a concept, it seems to me, that is in direct conflict with a religious and ethical tradition in which the human race is presented with 'a blessing and a curse, life and death', and we are instructed … therefore, to choose

life'. I believe euthanasia lies outside the commonly held life-centered values of the West and cannot be allowed without incurring great social and personal tragedy. This is not merely an intellectual conundrum ... This issue involves actual human beings at risk.[37]

Artificial Insemination

As stated earlier, science and medicine have developed great medical and surgical techniques in their efforts to sustain life. At the same time, science has also gravitated toward seeking out ways to generate life through medical procedures, namely artificial insemination. Along with the process of artificial insemination, however, come the arguments as to whether or not such a practice is ethical and moral. Contemporary critics might ask, for the sake of satisfying alien rights of the people, scientific inquiry, and the public's fanciful interest, how far are medicine and the legal system willing to push the boundaries of morality?

For example, "Recently a couple in the United States deliberately attempted to ensure the birth of a deaf child via artificial insemination ... the woman sees herself as no different from parent's trying to have a girl. She claims that girls can be discriminated against the same as deaf people and black people have harder lives."[38]

Judging from this couple's logic, they compared themselves to a minority group and see nothing wrong with attempting to place themselves in an identifiable group. In such a case, an investigation is needed to determine if this couple is using the option of artificial insemination as a means to satisfy their own sociopolitical views or if they genuinely want this to become a reality. In my judgment, it would serve humanity best if the court were to make a motion to diagnostically test and measure this couple's ability to make a rational and sound decision. But then again, the ACLU would make accusations of singling out this couple's right to make such a decision.

The issue of a woman's inherent God-given ability to procreate should not be construed as a license to abuse that gift. Life can be very taxing even for those who have all their mental wits and normal physical faculties about them let alone being intentionally burdened by deafness. Why anyone would choose to secure the birth of a deaf child simply to prove a point is incomprehensible. This is especially true if the couple is minimizing or inconsiderate of the social and functional problems that their deaf child would face, not to mention related emotional pain once the child becomes cognizant of his parent's actions. Without a doubt, the child could not help feel used and abused. The question is, are attempts to have an impaired child justifiable and should they be granted the same consideration as any other insemination case?

Given the level of legal intensity of any such cases, until a set standard of law is clearly defined, legal resolution of such delicate matters will not be handled in a blanket way. Each case will be subject to the moral conviction and legal interpretation by the judge who presides and how he or she views matters of artificial insemination. There are also the issues of various groups who represent both sides of the technological reproductive argument. Some of this argument stems from the feminist positions found in the "perspective of liberal Marxist, radical and cultural feminists, which to say from every angle one could imagine."[39] Because there does not appear to be a consensus or philosophical commonality among these groups, the likelihood of legal, ethical, and moral resolution will remain in a state of flux.

As if there aren't enough issues to contend with, artificial insemination has now reached a new level in the matter of posthumous sperm retrieval. In the article "Ethical Issues involved in Posthumous Sperm Retrieval," R.D. Orr and M. Siegler state, "It is possible to retrieve viable sperm from a dying man or from a recently dead body ... but the technical feasibility alone does not morally justify such an endeavor. Posthumous semen retrieval raises questions about consent, the respectful treatment of the dead body, and the welfare of the child to be."[40]

From my point of view, I firmly believe that any legal determination of euthanasia and artificial insemination should emphatically include a diagnostic review of the psychological and moral status of the person wanting to employ such practices. Again, this of course would stir the gander of every liberal ACLU attorney in the world.

Where reproductive technologies are headed leaves much to the imagination, but changes in man-made laws will lead the way to accommodate the ensuing ways of technological reproduction. For years to come, the courts will be challenged by the legal complexities brought on by euthanasia and artificial insemination.

Homosexuality and Same-Sex Marriages

Same-sex marriage and homosexuality are extremely delicate issues and far too complicated to address in a short presentation. But I do know that rather than be treated as a preference; both issues have become a political issue. Should you be inclined to pursue this topic in greater detail, the following articles may help you to gain a broader perceptive on this controversial topic: James Kirchick, "The New Religious Right," Advocate, Issue 1022, January 18, 2008, 40-43; State Legislatures,

Defense Marriage Act of 1998, Volume 36, 31-33; Emily Gill & Julia Mierzwa, "The First Amendment's Context: Religion Clauses and Same Sex Marriage," Conference Papers. 2008, 1-24; Nancy Wadsworth, "Intersectionality in California's Same Sex Marriage Battles," Political Research Quarterly, Volume 64, Issue 1, March 1, 2011, 200-216. In your own research you will discover that there are a vast number of articles with so much to say about most every aspect of this topic.

I created this chapter purposely to show some but certainly not all of the issues that characterize how man's thinking and judgment have overstepped the boundaries of morality and ethics. One has to ask how desires, beliefs, and emotions have gotten to this point. One explanation is more than adequate. There is a new worldview far removed from the Judaic-Christian doctrines that once were the sounding board for living and resolving problems. In its place is reliance on the courts and self more than reliance on God. 2 Timothy 3:2-7 warned of this day: "For men shall be lovers of own selves, covetous, boasters, proud, blasphemers, disobedient to parts, to parents, to parents, unthankful, unholy, without natural affection, truce breakers, false accusers, incontinent, fierce, despisers of those that are good, traitors, heady, high minded, lovers of pleasure more than lovers of God, having a form of godliness, but denying the powers thereof: from such turn away, for of this sort are they which creep onto houses, and lead captive silly women laden with sins, led away divers lusts, ever learning, and never able to come to the knowledge of truth."[41]

At this time I cannot help but interject two quotes from John Warwick Montgomery's book *The Shaping of America*. The first one is by a gentleman named Bruckberger. He is talking about the crumbling of certain aspects of society and asks the question where will the answer come if not from religion? He states, "Perhaps what the western world most lacks today is a clear and wholly comprehensible doctrine of man's earthly salvation, a doctrine not opposed to Christianity but inspired by it."[42] The second is from Picard's rally cry to his fellow German's after the fall of the Third Reich. He says, "There must be restored to the Germans an inner continuity, an inner personal history, and a center of personality where the good can dwell lastingly, independent from external elements."[43] In conjunction with the importance of practicing and saving Christian values, Picard's view has actually been my point throughout the book.

Closing out this chapter I would like to add that I personally have noticed that whenever antichristian groups succeed in defying anything Christian, boastfully it is acclaimed as a "boulder ripple effect" or "in your face milestone." It also seems there is something dramatically wrong when a nighttime television host announces the approval of "gay marriage" for a particular U.S. state and the audience applauds. Given the contents of this chapter, it is easy to see what the future of a Christian conscience will be if Christians do not stand up as a unified force and defend Christian doctrine.

VI

LIVING WITHOUT COVENANT-CAN AMERICA AND CHRISTIANITY SURVIVE?

Examining the definitive purpose for America's Declaration of Independence and The Constitution of the United States we find that they were developed to forge a new nation, free of England's tyrannical violation of human rights. But because the daring truths of America's founding fathers are rarely taught in today's public schools, the evolution of a tyrannically styled political governing representation, along with new age thinkers, have successfully won over the naiveté held by citizenry and the youthful uniformed and misinformed minds of America. The implications of this dramatic shift in thinking and its effects on Christian doctrine are the controlling premise for this chapter.

Historically, religion has played a major role in the development of America and for those of us who have made a commitment to Christ, regardless of the pitfalls of change and its attacks on morality and Christianity; we know that Jesus Christ is the Son of God and the pathway for our salvation to his grace. Beyond the principle of faith, this precept is also discernible through a surmountable and undisputable preponderance of spiritual and physical evidence listed in scripture. However, more than ever these truths are in jeopardy because of the self-indulgent character of society and various anti-Christian groups who diligently work to discredit and eliminate the written Word of God. An even greater threat is the interference and decisions by civil courts that legitimize specific agendas for various lobbyist groups who have no interest in the virtuous boundaries of God's expectations. These are the unbelievers who are entwined with the turbulence of self-indulgence, with little knowledge or concern for the immoral choices that will affect them for eternity. This irresponsible behavior is clearly referenced in Job 8:13. "So are the paths of all those that forget God; and the hypocrites hope shall perish."[1] This is referenced even deeper by the words of Jesus in John 6:63. "It is the spirit that quickeneth; the flesh profiteth nothing: the words that I speak unto you, they are spirit, and they are life"[2]

As stated earlier, when one thinks in terms of personal progress, it takes a great deal of effort and discipline to change a habit or conquer a crystallized addiction. This is especially true if the individual considers the addiction to be a comfort zone. Should this be the case, meeting the demands found in the consociation of Christian doctrine would be most difficult. To receive God's words, religion and spirituality cannot be viewed merely as intangible items otherwise the pleasurable tangibles of self-indulgence will certainly prevail. This social upheaval is exacerbated by Satan's involvement. He encourages not giving up the indulgences of life to believe in something unseen. Once again, Matthew 6:21 clearly delineate this repugnancy, "For where your treasure is, there will your heart be also."[3]

Given the new age way of thinking, dysfunctionality within the sphere of family circles is generally brought on by parents who by virtue of their own immorality and absence of God cause their children to search for love and attention elsewhere. America has lost sight of the fact that it is the parent's obligation to teach the children the things of God so that the children live in accordance to virtue rather than deceit; Proverbs 22:6 says, "Train up a child in the way he should go: and when he is old, he will not depart from it."[4]

Through the errors and neglect of parents and the psychological components of peer pressure, the moral and economic price that society pays is staggering. In my opinion, the influences of violent television, violent motion pictures, immoral theatrical dance and plays, video games with horrific content and perversity, and extremely poor role modeling by political leaders all have something to do with social breakdown and turning from God. Every cornerstone of common decency is affected by these various medias, and political correctness is getting in the way of Christian teachings, the first and best defense for correcting character deficits.

Insensitivity, child pornography, sense of entitlement, continual reliance on and abuse of social welfare, and inexcusable arrogance toward the principles of accountability and responsibility were never intended to be part of the moral fiber of America. America was primarily built on hardworking Christian people who had run from governmental tyranny. But in today's America we see a different breed of American. Intrusion by and reliance on government has created a sense of entitlement and a population that resents those of good moral conscience and as getting in the way of rightful governmental handouts. Detached from the Christian mainstream America, these lackluster individuals usually fall prey to

Satanism, cults, sects, and other anti-Christian movements that condone condemnation of Christian principles. In Matthew 7:15 Jesus makes clear the distinctions of "smoke and mirrored good": "Beware of false prophets, which come to you in sheep's clothing, but inwardly they are ravening wolves."[5]

Having surveyed some of the major contributors for biblical defection, we can see that no one particular source is clearly to blame for Christianity's problems. It is a combination of many things including false prophets, such as Jim Jones, reckless judicial prudence bending to an ant-Christian agenda, various religious cults, anti-Christian arguments from the American Civil Liberties Union, political correctness, reckless use of racism as a political weapon, and controversial anti-Christian House Bills written and passed with the support of anti-Christian political representatives and judges. I would go as far to say that even some Christian denominations have changed their positions on God's absolute law. The eminent danger from all these legal and immoral intrusions, especially those from the government, is that history speaks for itself when evaluating the political policies used in the persecution of Christians. Case in point, America's president is on record saying that "we are no longer a Christian nation" and "least we forget all the contributions the Muslims have made to the birth of this nation and the development of NASA space program." Frankly, I have never heard of nor am I aware of any Muslim contingencies riding horse-back across the great plains of Kansas. Not to be taken lightly, a modern-day list of infractions against Christianity by the government, civil courts, and the private sector would be voluminous. As stated earlier, "Perhaps what the Western world most lacks today is a clear and wholly comprehensible doctrine of man's earthly salvation, a doctrine not opposed to Christianity but inspired by it."[6] Better yet, it appears the president needs to repeat United States History 101.

While the anti-Christian movement works its political magic, there are Christian fundamentalist preachers who openly condemn the acts of government and those organizations that are purposely bent on destroying various elements of Christian ideology. But in my opinion one of the most dangerous of the antichristian movements is that of reckless and appeasing judicial prudence. For example, when someone complained that nativity scenes are offensive, the ACLU convinced the court that nativity scenes are offensive in public places or near public places. The court ruled in favor of the ACLU. This is but one ruling that accounts for the scarcity of nativity scenes during the celebration of Jesus' birth. Next on the scene come the constricting guidelines of political correctness. Political correctness has taken the Christ out of Christmas and substituted "Merry Christmas" with "Happy Holidays." In fear of being sued, product merchandisers and the Salvation Army followed suit. Even the Judaic Ten Commandments are no longer welcome in many places. School prayer has been long gone and churches no longer leave their doors open in fear of theft, destruction, and satanic reprisal. If the judiciaries would understand the role and reason they have been lifted, they would take their role more serious and understand that "even as they did not like to retain God in their knowledge, God gave them over to a reprobate mind, to do those things which are not convenient."[7]

Incontestably, preoccupation with self-indulgence has been and remains the breeding ground for modern-day man's repulsive attitude toward even the slightest hint of repentance. Not only does he refuse to repent, he rejects the empirical evidence for his spiritual ignorance. Essentially, there are many causal analogies that have contributed to man's spiritual death but one particular element is cited in 1 Corinthians 2:14: "But the natural man receiveth not the things of the Spirit of God: for they are foolishness unto him: neither can he know them, because they are spiritually discerned."[8] As much as one would like to make excuses or proclaim "I didn't know," we know for certain that St. Peter's denial wreaked mental havoc on him for the rest of his life.

Due to the current state of social conscience, it is not politically correct to mention spiritual things in a social context, especially in the work place. But how does one spread the gospel if they are ashamed, frightened, or restricted in their preaching the word of God? In matters such as these, should we as Christians lean on the guidance of Ecclesiastes 3:1 and pick and choose the battles we need to fight: "To every thing there is a season, and a time to every purpose under the heaven."[9]

Whatever avenue one should use to spread the gospel, the previous paragraphs are not intended to merely quote various Biblical passages to fill the page. The aforementioned anti-Christian examples are but a few and we Christians must realize that as Christians, we are obligated to fill the requirements of God's covenant. But in order to understand God's covenant, one must accept that there is a void in his or her life and believe that only God can fill the void of an empty soul. This realization is important because for an uneasy conscience, mental health therapeutic interventions can only change behavior but do very little to change the heart. The implication here is that Jesus Christ is the answer. He is the One "who heals all thine inequities; who healeth all thy diseases."[10] Secondly, if the reader assumes a position of interest with the slightest posture of faithful inquiry, the Holy Spirit will awaken that person to understanding the benefits from studying the moral and ethical doctrine of Christianity. With that being said, I want to move on to discussing God's covenant from both the Old and New Testament.

Exodus 2:23 states, "And it came to pass in process of time that the king of Egypt died: and the children of Israel sighed by reason of the bondage, and they cried, and their cry came up unto God by reason of the bondage."[11] From a position of faith, this verse validates that when people pray God listens and delivers. In the context of this promise, this certainly opens the door for deeper hermeneutical and theological debate.

In Genesis 1:29 it states, "And God said, behold I have given you every herb bearing seed, which is upon the face of all the earth, and every tree, in which is the fruit of a yielding seed; to you it shall be for meat."[12] Was this God's indirect way of committing to a covenant with man so as to ensure His relationship with man or did His covenant begin when He first decided to make the heavens and earth, knowing in His heart that man was soon to follow? Is it possible that God's first covenant with man could have been the very moment and act of His making man in His own image with Adam being conscious of the circumstances surrounding the forbidden fruit warning from God? Of certain, since Adam and Eve were cognizant of God's warnings, the choice to breach their commitment to God is definitely the first incident where man's journey toward preservation of self took place. At that very moment, man's fall from God's benevolence and initial intention for creations' synthesis with God was separated from natural harmony and balance. Balance was replaced by selfishness and acts of disobedience. What we see now is nonchalant acts of random murder, lying, stealing, infidelity, adultery, and many other abominations described and looked down upon by the Lord. Adam and Eve's fall is paralleled with the proclamation cited in Isaiah 44:10: "Who has formed a god, or molten graven image that is profitable for nothing."[13]

Even with Adam and Eve's disobedience toward God's commandment not to eat from the Tree of Knowledge of Good and Evil, God's grace toward man can still be seen when Adam and Eve realized that they were naked and fabricated aprons made of fig leaves. Genesis 3:21 states, "Unto Adam also and his wife did the Lord God make coats of skins, and clothed them."[14] This is another example of God's love and covenant with man. But even so, because of the good and evil Adam and Eve uncovered, they were sentenced to the fields of toil where promises of reward and punishment would always be governed by choice.

When analyzing the depth of the garden story, how do we know that Adam was not intrinsically conscious of his relationship with God? I say Adam was aware because God made man in His image and likeness, which presupposes an in place synthesis between God and man. Evidence for this synthesis is stated in Genesis 1:26: "And God said, 'Let us make man in our image, after our likeness: and let them have dominion over the fish of the sea, and over the fowl of the air, and over the cattle, and over the earth, and over every creeping thing that creepeth upon the earth.'"[15] True in every respect, then moving from right to wrong is definitely governed by a conscionable choice.

No doubt the book of Genesis tells of creation and the ordering of existence out of nothing, but a good starting point for identifying one of the first formal mentions of God's definitive promising covenant with man is stated and portrayed in Genesis 6:18. God spoke to Noah saying, "But with thee I will establish my covenant and thou shalt come into the ark, thou, and thy sons, and thy wife, and thy sons' wives with thee."[16] This covenant, however, does not exempt man from experiencing the constant pangs of suffering that culminate from a chosen path of disobedience and sin.

One would think that after the historic display of God's awesome power the world would be humbled and not revert back to old ways once a storm has passed. Yes, God does seek vengeance, but He also rewards repentance. In fact, God's own repentance is exemplified in Genesis 8:21 when He says, "And the Lord smelled a sweet savour; and the Lord said in his heart, I will not again curse the ground any more for man's sake; for the imagination of man's heart is evil from his youth; neither will I again smite any more every thing living, as I have done."[17] Knowing this, could this be man's preconceived insurance policy against God's beckoning?

Someone who is seeking God might ask if God truly made a covenant with man, what is it that I need to do to find Him? Scripture says, "If any man will come after me, let him deny himself, and take up his cross, and follow me."[18] But because self-indulgence rules, it is not easy to give up possessions to come to God even though embracing the kingdom of God guarantees eternal fulfillment: "But seek ye first the kingdom of God, and his righteousness; and all these things shall be added unto you"[19]

In a personal quest to know God, one of the best places to start would be to build upon a lifestyle according to God's expectations as spelled out in His Ten Commandments. Here God gives the most basic of all His requirements, and it is the pivotal point by which man can redeem himself and turn to a God-like way of life. However, reading of such things is one thing, living them is where the labor lives. But the choice to make a genuine and sincere effort is worth at least something in God's eyes because, "Of the righteous scarcely be saved, where shall the ungodly and sinner appear?"[20]

The essential principles of this book are built upon the strength and teachings of Scripture and what God expects from the followers of Christ. It is from this premise I conclude that liberalism and biblical defection are major contributors to America's moral decay. Both elements have stolen the respect and dignity that once were the backbone of our nation. It is also my contention that one of the most dangerous attacks to the survival of God-fearing, law abiding citizens is liberalism's quest to outlaw all guns, which is exactly why Christians should "cling to their guns and religion." Reasons to outlaw guns are pathetically shallow and set a dangerous precedent because "in an evil world force will always be necessary to restrain evil persons. Ideally, killings by police and military should not be necessary, but this is not an ideal world – it is an evil world. Ideally, we should not need locks on our doors or prisons. But it is simply unrealistic to assume we can get along without them in this wicked world."[21] This is especially true in that the founding fathers warned of potentially rogue government takeovers.

If we were to compare now with the times immediately following World War II, we would see that for the most part, American ideology was cohesive. There was a preoccupation with fulfilling the America dream through hard work and believing in the moral principles that historically gave this country its strength. But for a number of political and sociological reasons we have strayed from this course and have chosen the very same paths that brought other great civilizations to their knees. Essentially, America is economically and morally bankrupt and knowingly playing Russian roulette through its self-serving political representatives and pleasure seeking populace. This is especially true in the pop culture of illicit drug use. Thus far, if Americans have acquired a taste for drugs, other than personal responsibility, much to blame is the Federal Government who is charged with protecting the sovereignty of America's borders. But since God has been taken out of the equation and with personal political agenda more important, the resulting reality is runaway apathy, ignorance, and reliance on a "finger in the dike" style of government.

One step further, what can be said about the people who allow anti-Christian lobbyists to attack God through the courts? Initiative has been replaced by national complacency and a sense of entitlement. Guidance has been replaced with "live and let live." Rather than getting involved has been replaced by, "as long as it doesn't infringe on what I'm doing, that's okay." The traditional pillars of marriage, family unity, and fidelity have been reduced to a much lesser role in society. More disturbing is the irresponsible surge of out of wedlock children and resulting abortion that cheapens the value of God's gift of life. We can thank some of this to early sex education in schools. Faithfulness, moral values, and the blood covenant of Christ have been slandered by the sinful pleasure seeking masses that willfully pass personal responsibility onto a faltering government.

Although my perspective about the state of the nation are critical, I would go as far to say at least they are God oriented and consistent with sampling realty through logical processes far away from anti-American sentiment. For instance, who can deny that by overt policy the current trend is to covertly make as many people reliant on government? I can not overstress the fact that some of the methods used to achieve this goal are dangerous infringements on legal and religious rights and well outside the perimeters of prescribed jurisdiction of constitutional government. Sadly, certain members of Congress and the Christian masses, along with the general populace, have taken these infringements in stride. If allowed to continue, apathy will very well be the procuring cause for the end of many of our freedoms and religious practices in America. Astonishingly, two-thousand years later Jesus Christ is still denounced and a misinformed and uniformed populace places undying allegiance to political promises of change from recycled self-absorbed politicians in empty suits. Once more, the distinctive guidelines and interpretations of the meaning of change were never revealed, nor were they questioned by the majority of the voting populace. Having not learned from the false promises of change, voters are now getting in line cajoled by the mantra of "Forward." The question is, forward to what – more of the same? Scripture warns of false God's and indiscriminate leadership but the masses follow charismatic political shepherd's like sheep led to a cliff.

Expecting great things from the revision of traditional socio-economic and political structures, in the process, the masses did not consider that they might be giving up everything the original settlers and forefathers intended, which includes the freedom to do and achieve most anything possible absent of governmental intrusion. It is my fervent belief that one of the main reasons why the political mantra "change" was so readily accepted in the last election is that traditional American history has been eliminated from school curriculum. Subsequently, the current generation does not have a basic understanding as to what it took to make America a constitutional nation. They were never taught that struggling through the arduous task of day-to-day survival and the enormous probability for life-threatening retribution from King George, the original framers signed the Declaration of Independence so generations thereafter would live as free men. It has all been handed down to us and we were supposed to be keepers of the gate so the next generation could enjoy the same freedoms as the last. But what happened to the ideas of homogeneity and America's sovereignty as set forth by the constitutionalists? It is being transformed into something unrecognizable and surely not in the best interest of the American people. The distinct sounds of an ongoing political molestation and extirpation of Lady Liberty by the hands of unscrupulous politicians and liberal educators are evident.

Putting aside any misgivings I say it is the deadly combination of self-serving members of the House of Representatives, destructive presidential economic policies, indebtedness to lobbyists, the destructive tendencies of left-wing radicals, and an apathetic constituency, all contributing to America's political, economic and moral transformation. Here within breeds the pronounced drift from the basic formatted ideas of the free-market, Constitutional freedoms and dictates, and the role that a Christian God would play in America's future as a free capitalistic society. "The heart is deceitful above all things, and desperately wicked: who can know it?"[22]

From an economic standpoint, an example of blatant economic misrepresentation is seen in the rushed through congress "save the nation stimulus money." Without economic studies and against all advice from economists, trillions of dollars were hurriedly allocated on the pretext the government would otherwise collapse. The truth of the matter is the stimulus program did not have America's best interest at heart and did very little, if anything, to stimulate the economy as predicted. Overall, because the stimulus programs are essentially contrary to good economic sense, the only explanation is that they were deliberately designed and intended to destroy the free-market and ensure America's inability to recover from such horrendous indebtedness. By doing so, capitalist America would become economically defunct and restructured; thereby making the populace government reliant. If this is hard to fathom, why are there so many poor economic reports even after multi-trillion dollar economic stimulus programs? Why is America struggling to recover? Why are the same unemployment figures and gross national product figures hovering around the same percentage points when all indicators are clearly otherwise? If the real estate market appears to be on the rise, it's only because investors are buying up all the foreclosures. Are all these poor economic policies still George Bush's fault? Never has America allocated such enormous sums of money with virtually so little in return.

By this time you have to be asking what does the misrepresentation and misappropriation of economic funding have to do with the moral and spiritual soundness of our nation or the purpose for this book. It is my opinion that my idea of a sound nation is one where its leaders have a belief in God so making unconscionable decisions does not become a way of life. Without hesitation, I say that without a belief in God there is no future for America especially since it is prophesized, "And if a kingdom be divided against itself, that kingdom cannot stand".[23]

Evidence of these prophetic words can be seen in every aspect and dark corner of America's social problems. The wishful thinking of a "melting pot" has turned into a "smelly pot" absent of a clear homogeneous perspective as to where America should go as a nation. Instead of promised togetherness, our nation has been intentionally and grossly divided. The leaders and welfare recipients of this nation better come to grips with the reality that America does not have an infinite purse from which to draw upon. No better examples are the economic crumbling of Greece and other European socialist countries. Eventually, massive retirement packages, the fraudulent abuse of welfare programs, and "pork" related constituent projects will bankrupt America. This is exactly why America's sleeping citizen's need to get involved and question what political representatives are doing behind closed doors. You would be amazed to find that our representatives have forgotten their fundamental role as elected officials and have become political defalcators savoring the acquisition of power - not to serve, but to rule and to change.

Benefiting from the new boundaries of America's transformation are the festering cultivated poisons of political correctness, which has everything to do with indoctrination and silencing individual opinion. In my opinion the residual from the dictates of repressive political correctness greatly contributes to the development of a weak and fearful psychological profile. Thus, in the long run, and without opposition, moral biblical constraints will become legally obsolete and the laws that constrict free speech but protect immorality will certainly have unimpeded reign. In the truest sense, the moral integrity and political and religious cohesiveness of our country will cease to exist. America cannot survive such obtrusive constitutional and biblical damnation. This is why citizens need to stand firm in their Christian beliefs: "Beware of false prophets, who come to you in sheep's clothing, but inwardly they are ravening wolves."[24]

While this political coup moves forward with its anti-American agenda, the naïve are standing in the wings yelling, "They can't do that, it's a violation of our Constitutional rights." Where we go amiss is we fail to understand that America's constitution is a contractual agreement between the people and the elected and appointed government officials, the Supreme Court included, sworn to uphold and honor its stipulations. Under the current administration we are involved with an exercise in interpretive futility.

Given the circumstances, and for a number of reasons, it is only fair from here on out to refer to our leaders as misrepresentatives because under the slogan of "change", this new axis of power has promised to take us to the top of the mountain yet they themselves are seated in the deceitful valley of narcissistic existential political absurdity. Even at the cost of destroying the economic and moral infrastructure of this great nation, there are those representatives that still find it politically safer to get on board with the proponents for change rather than doing the right thing to do.

Since her conception, America has gone through some rather distinct social and political transformations but the last presidential election harbors a political social transformation unlike anything America has ever seen. In most every key appointed position are heads of office that clearly have their roots in a leftist anti-American agenda. Contributing to this modern day coup d'etat, Republican house members, for the most part, have been silent in their political objection to this macabre administration, which in my opinion makes them an equal partner and accessory to this criminal circus. It is also my opinion that had it not been for the true conservative rookie Tea Party congressional members, the Republican Party was ready to concede to defeat. But even so, the social and political hallmarks that brought America to its greatness are still in jeopardy. There is much at stake in the 2012 election.

Equally contributing to this political insurrection are the misinformed and uniformed voters, who in their naiveté, can not see through the overall political connotation and implication of the word change. They assumed that change meant America finally buried the hatchet of racism and earnestly could vote for a half-black man for President. Much to their surprise, heart felt change has brought nothing but higher taxes, wasteful spending, massive debt, efforts to redistribute wealth under Marxist "fairness" ideology, implementation of policies that knowingly would destroy the independent small businessman, implementation of programs that discourage economic growth, an increase of America's military vulnerability, a relentless effort to character assassinate political opposition by whatever means possible, and the destruction of all the issues and headway Dr. Martin Luther King fought for. Rather than calling Obama's destructive policies for what they are, at the slightest hint of objection, opposition is viewed as racism.

Blinded by a charismatic empty suit, voters went to the polls without doing their homework on a man who has a glaring lengthy history of associating with leftist anti-American political hooligans, some of which are deeply entrenched in Marxist ideals and hate for America. As a result, what we have now is an anti-American administration filled with left-winged politicians who have made it their life's work to destroy the free-market system of America and to replace it with government run institutions. Supporting this political takeover are the organized labor unions, a silent press, and the multicultural legal and illegal voters who haven't taken the time to learn the English language let alone the intricacies of American politics. Swayed by promises of government support, ballots are cast on the promise that the government will continue to give something for nothing. All this amounts too is selling the life-blood of the country for votes. It is very difficult for conservative ideals to compete with the promise of a free economic ride.

It is easy to discern that my opinion about how this administration's economic policies are purposely doing everything contrary to solid economic sense so as to destroy the free-market economy. The end result of this planned reformation could only mean satisfying the goal of a citizenry strangled by inept government run programming predicated on collectivism rather than the benefits of free-thinking individualism. Assuredly, the rejection of this assertion would only come from those mesmerized doltish voters who in the last election had experienced a messianic blessing. I submit to you that if the people who voted for liberal change would take the time to analyze the fruits from the failed and grossly misrepresented economic policies of the current administration, tingling sensations would be a thing of the past.

What are the pitfalls of socialist style of government? Take a good look at those European countries who are trying to reverse their own economic and political travesties derived from socialism. As with communism, socialism does not work to the benefits of all it purports to service. It largely benefits those at the top. Beyond the issue of power and control, in a socialist style of government leaders are delighted to wallow in their political and economic windfall even though those at the bottom spend their time grabbling for a living. It is my opinion that it's time to wake up and believe that America is on its way to meeting the criteria for a classic definition of a third world socialist country politically rooted in Marxist ideals. More than any other time in American history there is a need for multiple days of national prayer. But don't count on the president to participate.

As it stands now, our elected officials have the best health care and retirement package anyone could possibly imagine but apparently this is not enough. They want to fly around the world and drive everywhere with limousine entourages at taxpayer expense while preaching to you about conservation, global warming, and why you need to think "green." When politicians think green it has nothing to do with the environment. We would be hard pressed to find one political representative who would give up their golden parachute health care program to receive medical services through Obama care. I find it interesting that this medical manifesto is being forced on the American people but political representatives don't want any part of it. If it was good, politicians would not hesitate to get their fair share of the pie. In my opinion, I predict that conscionable doctors and health care professionals will abandon the medical field leaving the professionally inept and a defunct administrative system to provide medical services. More disturbingly, the manner in which the Supreme Court approved Obama care as constitutional, it says to me that under this administration, all America's sacred documents and institutions are either dead or dying. Sadly, on both sides of the isle, as a unit or separately, Congress, the president, and the Supreme Court are politically-unhealthily dysfunctional and out of control.

Count the ways, identify the origin, and you will see America is being politically transformed by a far left-winged power hungry group of elected and appointed officials who have a specific agenda; one that abridges the constitution without accountability. Again, this brazen disconcerting leadership only continues because of a frazzled congress and an undisciplined apathetic constituency who refuse to believe the truth right before their eyes. Subsequently, this unchecked political and social tsunami is eradicating freedoms for future generations. Veterans of all foreign wars have got to be turning over in their grave not to mention America's military who are currently fighting foreign wars. Compounding matters, it is quite obvious that the guardians of our constitution are in total disarray and have an agenda of their own.

For those who believe in the hallowed principles of America and the guiding principles of Christian doctrine, current reformations are not simply the sign of changing times. These are all signs of biblical prophesied end times. Aware of these preliminary travesties, Christian solace lies in the conscious thought of the second coming of Christ and not in chameleon politicians who promise great things if elected. Believers also revere that as a theological truth and guide from damnation, scripture speaks for itself and it is up to each individual to choose which side of this reality they will live. Foremost, Christians believe and know that Jesus Christ truly is the Son of God and the only way to heaven's salvation.

Without question, America's strength is recorded as being rooted in those leaders and individuals who adhered to Christian principles. Nevertheless, these principles are currently under attack from left-wing anti-Christian God and anti-American disciples; many of which are in the arenas of Hollywood, uneducated talk show hosts, and paparazzo television panels fronted by cosmetically adorned harlequins.

As long as the destructive tendencies of left-wing opposition continue to have free reign, America will certainly be at odds with raising its children in the traditional sense of the word. In fact, Sweden is experiencing one such social transformation. The Swedish government is advocating and enforcing that from the age of one, children should be placed in state-run day care centers. The implication here is the government can raise and teach your children better than you. What government proposes to teach is the question. This governmental intrusion on freedom is uprooting conscientious Swedish families and causing them to move to neighboring Finland.

When we look at the current transformation of America there are some definitive social factors that have greatly contributed to the beginning of its ruination. From the hippie sixties came the burning of bras and the movement of woman's quest for equality. But in the process, women inadvertently aborted chivalry and now find themselves opening doors and suffering the same stress related illnesses that only men have been known to experience. In an attempt to recapture the feminine persona associated with the past, in all age groups skirts have gotten tighter and shorter and there is a mad dash for cosmetic bosomy. In the political realm, politicians have gotten more brazenly corrupt and have sold America's ingenuity to foreign countries for personal gain by virtue and influence of political position. Crimes in every spectrum of society have gotten more heinous and punishment more lenient. CEO's are less trustworthy, sexuality is more descriptive and loose than ever, and adult and child pornography is rampant. Aside from the break down of moral decency we have the hypocrisy and failed policies of a malfunctioning billion dollar homeland security program, government's failure to enforce federal immigration laws and condemning those that do, Church leaders found to be unfaithful to duty as spiritual leaders, and the expectation for individuals to assimilate political correctness and believe the falsehoods of evolution, proven to be concocted global warming science, and "green" policies, which have gone nowhere. When there is an obvious Islamic terrorist act in America, political correctness dictates that we shouldn't jump to conclusions. According to this administration there are no Islamic terrorists, only insurgents. More disturbing are the rules of engagement our military has to contend with when dealing with Islamic terrorists. But on the other hand, government and the courts will attack Christian doctrine and go after any individual or Christian group that appears to be thinking against the grain of federal approval. Furthermore, what purpose does a police force serve in the war on terrorism if they cannot ask an individual if they are a citizen? Political correctness is jeopardizing the security and sovereignty of our country. Are we to assume that these changes are a sign of the times and the permeable proletariat should surrender to each new administration and the dictates of their damnation? If this is the case, then it appears John 5:19 is not too far off in its proclamation that, "the whole world is under control of the evil one."[25]

Because political representatives arrogantly separate themselves from the people, they can not be genuinely in tune with the needs and minds of the people. A classic example is their perception of racism. Representatives are under the notion that racism can be irradiated through political rhetoric and legislation, which has nothing to do with what's in a man's heart. The only way to minimize the pitfalls of such indignities is to change the hearts and minds of men; the place where God has been systematically eliminated and blasphemed by anti-God lobbyists and the liberal courts. Adding greater fuel to this anti-Christian and anti-American movement we have a president who says that America needs to apologize for all the international atrocities we have committed. How can this be? Aside from the trillions of dollars America has donated to feeding the world she has given the lives of countless young American men and women who fought and continue to fight to save the world from tyrannical dictators. What's to apologize for? If this is the case then America should apologize to King George's descendants for treason against mother England. To the contrary, the original settlers who founded America ran from religious persecution and founded this country on basic Christian principles, which have been the very religious core of our beloved America for over two hundred years. Clearly, we are a nation whose fundamental religious premise is based on Christian doctrine. In fact, several previous Presidents were ordained Christian ministers. In addition, there are hundreds of documents where officials of our government have stated or referred to America as being a Christian nation.

In every sense of the word, America is a Christian nation just as much as Islamic countries profess to be Islamic nations and Israel priding itself as a Jewish nation. In fact, all throughout many of America's constitutional documents, court rulings, as well in various presidential official and personal beliefs, we see cited evidence that America's roots are based off Christian doctrine. On July 4th, 2012 I found some examples of this contention on a website called, USA Christian Ministries. There were several listed but one of the most glaring can be found in the words of the First Amendment:

> "Done in Convention by the Unanimous Consent of the States present the Seventh Day of September in the Year of our Lord one thousand seven hundred and Eighty-seven and of the Independence of the United States of America the Twelfth...." Because the Lord of Christianity is Jesus Christ, this makes America a Christian nation. Another prominent display of recognizing America as a Christian nation can be seen in the Supreme Court ruling in the Church of the Holy Trinity v. United States, 1892. It was determined by the Supreme Court that:

> "Our laws and our institutions must necessarily be based upon and embody the teachings of the Redeemer of mankind. It is impossible that it should be otherwise; and in this sense and to this extent our civilization and our institutions are emphatically Christian...This is a Christian nation."

Harry S. Truman believed that:

> "The fundamental basis of this Nation's law was given to Moses on the Mount. The fundamental basis of our Bill of Rights comes from the teachings which we get from Exodus and St. Matthew, from Isaiah and St. Paul."

Calvin Coolidge is quoted as saying,

> "The foundations of our society and our government rest so much on the teachings of the Bible that it would be difficult to support them if faith in these teachings would cease to be practically universal in our country."

President Dwight D. Eisenhower stated:

> "Without God there could be no American form of
> government, nor an American way of life. Recognition
> of the Supreme Being is the first, the most basic, and
> expression of Americanism. Thus, the founding fathers of
> America saw it, and thus with God's help, it will continue
> to be."

Last but not least are the words of President Ronald Reagan:

> "The Bible and its teachings helped form the basis
> for the Founding Fathers' abiding belief in the inalienable
> rights of the individual, rights which they found implicit
> in the Bible's teachings of the inherent worth and dignity
> of each individual. This same sense of man patterned
> the convictions of those who framed the English system
> of law inherited by our own Nation, as well as the ideals
> set forth in the Declaration of Independence and the
> Constitution."

Up until lately, the matter of our nation as a Christian nation has always stood tall in the hearts and minds of America's leaders and the majority of its citizens. Compared to then, what we have now are unscrupulous anti-American leaders and various agencies working against every aspect of Christian doctrine. Their contention is that we are a nation of all religions. Granted, to a degree this is true because our founding documents allow for such religious practices, but the very founding of the nation has been proven to be based on Christian doctrine and principle. What the anti-Christian movement gives us are ideals that attack the very notion, which gives individual freedoms to all. They present their arguments in such a way that it appears they are working to preserve freedoms for all but in truth, they are trying to destroy any representation of what freedom truly stands for. For example, on their watch voter fraud is rampant and intentionally overlooked, the Pledge of Allegiance is under attack, words of the national anthem are questionable, school prayer has been eliminated, and children are taught the political venomous poison of left-wing anti-American propaganda. Beware, "For false Christs and false prophets shall rise, and shall shew signs and wonders, to seduce, if it were possible, even the elect."[26]

It is not coincidental that in line with Obama's announcement to the world that America is not a Christian nation; a national magazine headlines a front page article announcing the decline and fall of Christianity.

Categorically, these incidences fit right in with the premise of what this chapter professes – efforts to reshape and transform America unaligned with what the forefathers intended. No doubt in my mind the media is selling its ink to the highest bidder. Ironically, these leftist Punchinellos are instrumental in destroying the very hand that feeds them.

Caught up in a world of delusion, corruption, greed, kickbacks, and spiritual depravity, the political position of power is not solely the blame; the political position is merely the vehicle by which elected officials can employ what is already crystallized in their inner most wicked thoughts and behaviors. They do what they do because this is who they are. Essentially, they come to the House of Representatives with an agenda. What better place to feed the cravings for self-importance and personal economic gain than the realm of political position; that is, if you are without conscience and absent of Christian values.

There are many reasons why so many prevailing immoral and fraudulent acts are allowed to continue but there is only room enough to cite a few. But from my perspective, the following two are fairly conclusive. Uncontested, immorality has worked its way into prominence because of an apathetic and self-indulged society that simply has given up and blended into this way of life. The self-indulged find it much easier to live in a chosen literal sense than to live in fear of reprisal from an unseen higher power. Two, because the impact of the residual from failure to admonish benevolence has yet to fully surface, today's remnants of yesterday's neglect is in full blown operation and oblivious to the fact that there will come a day of reckoning. Only in the end will the anti-Christian followers know and fully understand the travesty of their neglect and what they have allowed to happen. In the end they will fully understand the prophecy of Romans 14:12. "So then, every one of us shall give account of himself to God."[27]

How can America get back on track? For starters, it would be beneficial if representatives would choose the moral codes of Christian doctrine over liberalism. This encompasses adherence to God's written laws rather than succumbing to Satan's dissuasion from goodness. Acceptance of both propositions is not possible. It must be either or. The populace must also realize that the political and moral direction of the country is not happenstance; it is part of a calculated plan to reshape America. This immoral and political reshaping of our nation only continues because good people stand by and do nothing as bad people continue to do bad things. The victims in governmental sublimation can be seen by the ulterior motives of lobbyists and political representatives who have "delegalized" God and made homosexuality a political issue rather than the private preferential issue that it is. How arrogant to defy our lawful God. America would be so much better off if we never allowed the American flag to touch the ground or to be wrapped and displayed in disrespectful ways.

Yes, times have changed and very little of today resembles America when morals and integrity were high. Maybe it still isn't too late. Maybe with God's blessing and the help of conscionable individuals from every race, creed, and color, we can turn this country around for the better. One sure way would be to thank God for the choice of repentance and His retributive Day of Judgment. Here truly lies the Supreme Court.

Epilogue

Throughout the book I meant to be rather critical about several issues that are sensitive to me, especially those related to the immoralities of our failing social structure induced by government and the attacks on Christian doctrine. These are legitimate concerns that need to be addressed not only by Christians but by anyone of a good moral conscience who believes in the American way of life. It is my personal solemn warning that America's survival depends on it. During the course of writing this book I also felt a need to express my personal opinions concerning the economic recklessness of the current administration and how it will effect generations to come. If America has to endure another four years of Obama's political and economic travesties, moving forward under the mantra of change, we will no longer celebrate July 4th as the birth of our nation. Instead, we will be subjected to the birth of a new nation, one unlike anything our founding fathers intended.

From the very beginning, I presented my commentary in such a way that it would awaken sleeping Christians and those Americans who refuse to believe that they have become disenfranchised by their own apathy. The facts of my research are presented as I discovered them. I did not have to manipulate the facts to shape a meaning or to develop a stronger argument for the book. In conjunction with my research findings, my contentions are straightforward and not contaminated by conjectures based on prejudice. Summed up, each chapter delineates the dispensation of the political upheaval and derailment of America's most fundamental political, economic, religious, and social foundations. In their simplest form, the moral failings and planned economic transformation of America I speak of is as clear as the American Revolution itself.

It is quite clear that Christianity has major problems generated from infighting. But more than anything, I can assure you that the impact on the realities of America's social upheaval can be traced more to the pivotal point of a disregard for Christian values, destructive left-wing politics, personal rather than Constitutionally based Supreme Court decisions, and collateral damage caused by reckless executive privilege. The failed repercussions from these agencies have impacted every aspect of America's moral and religious construct. I exercised a basic commitment to exposing these negative social infractions in my discussions about teaching evolution in schools rather than creation, the ACLU's involvement in eliminating various Christian symbols from public places, right to life issues, and what we can expect for the future of America if we are no longer a nation under a Christian God. The crux of my conclusions is that no good can come from a nation that represses the moral values of Christianity in its schools, institutions, social constructs, and those physical symbols that depict our Christian God. Historically, these agencies have been responsible for disseminating the rhetorical tools necessary for the preservation of America as one nation under God. But little by little they have been neutered from serving in that capacity. They are under attack from every which way imaginable. It is my opinion that the majority of the attacks are from evil forces absent of God. I say this because no leader in a God conscience would make such detrimental economic policies knowing all the while that they would have such an enormous negative impact on millions of innocent Americans. This is but one reason why I say that Christians from every denomination and Americans from every walk of life must come together. This is also why I say America needs to return to its Christian base. Disregard for Christian values has pushed the influential properties of moral civility, integrity, and ethics to an all time low. America cannot afford to lose much more of its traditional infrastructure to rogue forces otherwise we could very well lose the freedom to practice Christianity itself. It's happening in other countries and don't think it can't happen here.

Under the contrived political slogan "change", American's went to the polls assuming they were voting for the much awaited messiah. However, what these mislead constituents failed to do was question what the semantics and use of the word change would mean for America. I don't mean to gloat but even before his inauguration, my personal mantra about Barack Hussein Obama, was that he did not come to fix and build; he came to dismantle the traditional American way of life. This is clearly evidenced by his intentional destructive economic policies housed in unproductive stimulus programs, policies that discourage economic growth, enacting laws that would keep small businesses and corporations from hiring, not to mention the projected forthcoming failed outcomes from Obama care. Something is dramatically wrong with America's governmental ruling agencies, the Supreme Court included, when they can bless the articles of a bill, which very few have read in its entirety, including its writers. Worth mentioning again are the infamous words of House Speaker Nancy

Pelosi, "We have to pass this bill so we can see what's in it." The subsequent economic and political damage from this administration is like none other in the history of America. Should this anti-American group of individuals be reelected, America will be totally transformed into a government style resembling early 20th Century English guild socialism, one where the state owns and runs everything. One where there would be even greater retribution for Christianity and destruction of God rather than adoration. The likes of such leaders are described in scripture. 2 Corinthians11:13 warns, "For such are false prophets, deceitful workers, transforming themselves into apostles of Christ."[1] 2 Timothy 3:5 states, "Having a form of godliness, but denying the power thereof: from such turn away."[2] The question is where do we go from here?

Within each chapter I emphasized my opinion that many of America's problems are a direct result of placing the Christian God on the back burner and as having little, if any regard for His teachings. Much of this stems from new age thinking and governmental involvement in the repression of Christianity. There is also the philosophical notion that if there was a God, then none of the tribulations would be happening. This is so far from the truth because rather than look to the negative results generated by poor choices, living a Godless life makes it easier to blame and discredit a much adorned God. As a Christian, I find it mind-boggling that rather than trusting God's four thousand year recorded and proven history, citizens find it easier to incessantly relinquish their constitutional and God given rights to unscrupulous political misrepresentatives, many of which share in an absence of God. Given this set of circumstances, the only fair analysis I can offer for man's reason to exist is simply to prey on one another. By the looks of things, the dead and dying are everywhere.

The majority of my opinions held within the covers of this book derive from my love for Jesus and America, a lengthy interest in politics, and trying to understand man's inhumanity to man. In fact, ever since the fifth grade, I thought I wanted to be like President Lincoln. Later in life I discovered that I did not want to get caught up in supporting the livelihood of anti-American Hollywood celebrities, uneducated anti-American talk show hosts, and left-wing ideologists. I also learned that in the presentation of truth, it is not possible to satisfy all the people all the time, so why try? This accounts for my hard-line approach in examining and writing about the distortions and manipulations of our current administration to the degree that I have. I tried to be respectful but candid. I am quite confident that this is evidenced throughout the book. Scripture asserts that men such as myself are the men whose faith is, "not in the wisdom of men but in the power of God"[3]

No doubt, the particulars of such a broad spectrum of information can be cumbersome, which is why I purposely contextualized each comment along with suggesting in-depth cause and effect relationships. This is what any good elucidator would do. Philosophically, Edmond Hillary climbed mountains because they were there. I write because I am personally fed up with the ongoing political molestation and extirpation of Lady Liberty; much of which I strongly believe is caused by the deafening cadence of Biblical defection.

Wholeheartedly, my strategy was to build a strong enough argument to awaken all conscionable Americans to realize that there is both a hidden but obvious agenda for reshaping the goose that lays the golden egg. None of the reshaping has to do with positive reinforcement of the populace. It has everything to do with the development of an oligarchic power, seated in personal economic gain with absolute control over the populace. If you find this difficult to swallow, follow the money trail and you'll see that a large portion of the "much needed stimulus money" went to nonproductive entities with the cost of this economic give away to be felt in higher taxes for generations to come. From the get go, this move was extremely contrary to good economic sense and had everything to do with justifying an excuse for the dismantling and takeover of private and government sector institutions, some of which are already inept and structurally unsound due to corruption.

My rigorous scrutiny concerning the infertile polka dot behavior and malicious intent of some of our anti-American policy makers is not predicated on personal aggrandizement. I am not a futilitarian nor am I bounded by the dogma of Republicanism or Democratic principle. I've given up on these political organizations long ago because both parties, by choice, have abandoned the roots of who they are leaving America's original personification to an axis of entrenched self-serving left-wing political renegades who have nothing but contempt and distain for the ideology of what traditional America represents. Do you find this hard to believe? Well, take a good look at the countless attacks on our inalienable rights and the erosion of morality, freedom, and distain for anything that represents Christianity. Take a real good look at how the current administration is spending so far out of our means that we will be indebted for years to come and to who knows what lender. Take a look at how the current administration, in many areas, has exceeded Constitutional limits. This is not by accident; this is by collective design and an overt disregard and disrespect for the Constitution itself. Somewhere in the shadows hidden behind closed doors is a frightened and spineless Congress talking amongst themselves trying to find a way to fix what's happening to America without contributing to their own political demise. Worse yet, the damage this administration has inflicted on the American people may be irreparable. At this point in time, the beauty of America is that it gives me the freedom to voice my concerns and at the same time, allowing reciprocity for those in disagreement. But who knows what is waiting for America should this Anti-American political platform be granted another four years. So far, all we've gotten from "change" are a hapless fate and economic genocide.

If you are in tune with the distinct sounds of "change", you would know that these anti-American political ideas are real and are held in consort by a large segment of our political leaders in key positions and by left-winged constituents who have full knowledge but little concern for the long term implications of what they support. This new axis of power has promised to take us to the top of the mountain but where we are seated is in a valley close to death as one could get without dying.

Unlike any other time in American history, we have never experienced so much negative anti-Americanism from one administration. Rather than fulfilling the campaign promise of "togetherness", America is more divided than ever. We now have a left-wing political coup bent on destroying the infrastructure of America and the American people still haven't awakened from the sucker punch they voted for. The reality of this contention is seen in many different places and one in particular is the blatant abuse of "Executive Privilege" as an excuse not to give credence to America's Constitutional grievance process. According to Amendment I of the United States Constitution the American people have the right "to petition the government for a redress of grievances." Presently, there are legal attempts to satisfy the immeasurable contention whether or not we have a President who was born in America. Rather than assist in silencing this controversy once and for all, all records concerning this matter have been sealed. If there is nothing to hide, why seal the record? I say it's more than just having fun with political games taunting the Conservative block. If anything, something has gone amuck in the world of decency and common good, which is exactly why I feel our current government's convoluted reasoning qualifies for Emmanuel Kant's description and ideas about a noumenon; that which is known to exist but absent of intelligible properties.

I John 3:3 proclaims, "We are children of God."[4] I John 4:3 also warns that, "And every spirit that does not confess that Jesus Christ has come in the flesh is not of God. And this is the spirit of the Antichrist, which you have heard was coming, and is now already in the world."[5] Yes, the anti-Christ is here and he's making his presence felt by working his poison through the Godless hearts of the political left, the United Nations, and many other elements harboring an anti-American and anti-Christian agenda. The only saving grace from this anti-American movement will be going to the polls in record numbers and the American traditions of clinging to our guns and religion; the very premise by which this country was founded.

It is my belief that not all America's problems are due to government abuse and neglect. Americans as a whole have dropped the torch for carrying on with morality, integrity, personal responsibility, accountability, and defending the fundamental rights inherent in the U.S. Constitution and Bill of Rights. They are complacent and have punted individual responsibility to a faltering and corrupt government. Furthermore, scanning the House of Representatives it would be taxing to find a representative that could be considered a genuine role model. I might add that if a representative was truly working for America, America would not be in the predicament that it is. What this says to me is that the majority from both parties are all part of the overall plan to reconstruct America to accommodate the New World Order.

If constituents would take the time to question what their representatives were doing behind closed doors, representatives never would have obtained so much political power. This is exactly why I support term limits. Out of my own curiosity I've often wondered why politicians who proclaim, "I'm working for you" never became missionaries or pursued a career working for a charitable organization. This line of work would be more in line with what they expect you to believe about them. Instead, they've opted to go where the money is. But in the end, "For God shall bring every work into judgment, with every secret thing, whether it be good, or whether it be evil."[6]

In my opinion there is so much wrong with America that it's going to take a major effort by everyone to put her back on track. If it were up to me I'd start with our educational system because ala Islamic teachings, indoctrinations are best formulated at a very young age. Rather than teaching American history and emphasizing the value systems that propelled this country to its greatness, children are taught most everything anti-American, anti-Christian, and the evilness of the free market system. Children are also taught the benefits of "positive play", which in many respects is nothing more than transforming the psychological profile from individualism to collectivism during the early stages of development. By the time these individuals reach mid-school they will be indoctrinated into believing that it is not "fair" that they should develop or possess superior skills when others are less fortunate. There is also a trend to change the words and intent of long-standing nursery rhymes so as to make them positive with happy endings rather than sad. I can see it all now, "Old Mother Hubbard went to the cupboard to give her poor dog a bone, when she got there the cupboard was bare, but that's okay, the government will take care of all her needs." Better yet, "There once was a lady who lived in a shoe, she had so many children she didn't know what to do. But not to worry, she will get a government check for each and every one of her non-productive children. So keep up the good work." Let's not forget, "Humpty-Dumpty sat on a wall, Humpty-Dumpty had a great fall, all the king's horses and all the king's men put Humpty-Dumpty back together again because with Marxist collective group thinking, you could accomplish anything." The play on words for these nursery rhythms is humorous but the parallelisms of reality and truth concerning government takeover are no joke. In more ways than one America is in deep trouble.

By comparison, the America of today and the one that I knew are eons apart. For example, when I attended grade school in the early 1950's, each and every morning we started our day by singing the National Anthem, America the Beautiful, and then closed by reciting the Pledge of Allegiance. Today, we would be hard pressed to find any school that would give reverence to any one of these creeds. In some cases the likes of them are even excluded from public events. What we have now is more of an emphasis on bilingualism. Not that there is anything wrong with learning a new language but the irony of the bilingual focus is that the majority of students enter high school and college with major deficits in the English language, the most spoken language in the world and the mother tongue of America. Personally, I've often wondered why I have had to dial "1" for English over 35 years ago but now I know. It has been a planned political reformation, one where there is a built-in Democratic voting block for a population whose reward is to draw benefits from government assistance. In a similar fashion, extending and lowering education loan rates has nothing to do with creating jobs. It has everything to do with nurturing a youthful and naïve voting block that has yet to understand under this administration's ideas there will be no job waiting for them.

When I discussed some of the early history and pitfalls of Christian infighting I used this as a cue to draw attention to how ridiculous it is when there are more important issues at hand, largely the attacks on Christianity itself. With each post-war generation, new teachings have been coordinated with deeper and more frequent attacks on Christianity by senators, congressmen, and various anti-God lobbyist's who give no credence to the inclination that there is a God let alone live by His expectations. Even show biz celebrities are using their prominence to mislead audiences into believing that there are other ways to heaven besides Christ. Feeling comfortable and safe, the anti-Christian movements and nonbelievers will still lose in the long-run. Christ emphatically says, "I am the way, the truth, and the life. No one comes to the Father except through Me. If you had known Me, you would have known My Father also; and from now on you know Him and have seen Him."[7] This heart warming affirmation is significantly different in his warning that, "He who rejects Me, and does not receive My words, has that which judges him – the word that I have spoken will judge him in the last day."[8] As a believer I am not surprised by the obtrusive nature of the contemporary anti-Christian God and new age movement because this has been foretold in Psalm 14:1. "The fool hath said in his heart, there is no God. They are corrupt, they have done abominable works, there is none that doeth good"[9]

Also resonating throughout the book is my fervent belief that everything relative to use-to-be common sense has taken on the likes of bordering on insanity and perverted idealism. Rather than obedience to righteousness, at the forefront of living are deception, lies, and corruption. Political and corporate criminals at every level escape accountability, leadership allegiance to country is compromised, rather than protect the articles of America's Constitution, the Supreme Court has relinquished that role to party affiliation, and marriage between a man and a woman has lost its meaning as a God given Holy sacrament.

Looking back, there was a time when humans seemed to make a consorted effort to live up to their conscience recognizing and feeling the shame that culminates from shameful and immoral deeds. Anymore, it is not uncommon for governmental representatives to commit immoral and illegal acts without consideration for consequences or giving any thought to what their impact may have on America's moral image. Many representatives have been caught committing infractions on audio videotape and still have the audacity to deny their infraction because their behavior and words "have been taken out of context" or "what you see really isn't what you think it is." With Bible in hand, some parade through life looking for any photo opt that would record their piety. The irony of this moral decline is that these are the same political representatives who enact laws to control the behavior of the masses. In some cases these very same immoral misrepresentatives are canonized before their time. Crime is out of control and leadership is inept and wanting. Again, I intentionally call them misrepresentatives because the word leader has a specific connotation within the vernacular of worthiness. At the apex of all this perversion we currently have thousands of military men and women dying on foreign soil, while at the same time, the President knowingly making political and economic moves to destroy the longstanding capitalistic infrastructure of America, the very things these young men and women are literally dying to protect. In my opinion, there are no redemptive qualities in the current administration.

For a number of reasons I find it necessary to speak candidly about the state of our nation because all around me I see nothing but disparity from a populous craving for leadership free of lies and promises that never will be met. Uncontrolled change is dangerous. It's as though America is drunk with madness. Home foreclosures by the millions, families separated and divorced, millions of jobs lost to foreign countries, false promises by the president and never announcing corrective measures, government bailout of private and unionized industries, etc. More disheartening is the fact the very ideals that use to separate the two major political parties of this country are no longer identifiable. Rather than definitive idealistic lines, what we have now is a squiggly line, which signifies non-allegiance to either party thereby making it easier to cross over during a political trade-off.

To this extent I believe integrity, dignity, and the principalities of the word principle have evaporated. In its place evolved a self-serving communal hot tub with each party trading political allegiance like a branch of the New York Stock Exchange. To save faith, occasionally a few sacrificial lambs are encouraged to step down. Never before in the history of America have so many representatives, including the president, committed so much national destruction and sin without shame or accountability. Who dare say that this is not the case? In the Gospel of John 8:47 these Godless behaviors are clearly delineated for it is said, "He who is of God hears God's words; therefore you do not hear, because you are not of God.[10]

When I reflect back on my high school years, I rode a city bus to school. Above each window were advertisements selling everything imaginable. I remember one advertisement that always seemed to get my attention, which as a teen-ager was rather frightening. It was a picture of Nikita Khrushchev shaking his fist with a written connotation below stating, "We will bury you." Obviously that never happened but over time a new slogan emerged. China prophesized, "We will never have to attack you. You will destroy yourself from within." Who knows, maybe with their new found wealth in capitalism, they will have a better contextual understanding of the heart of America.

Since the conception of this great nation, the majority of its problems have always been solved by its people and not with smothering programs with a deluge of money or nationalization of its institutions. This is clearly evidenced in President Johnson's "Great Society." There are literally hundreds of Johnson's ideas still being funded and none can honestly say that they have put a dent in the social problems of America. From one administration to the next the scepter of power proclaims that they have the answer but all we keep getting are propagandized proclamations discussing the state of the economy and America's need to be independent of foreign oil.

In the most vigorous sense of understanding God, the source for my spiritual inspiration and contextual reliability largely comes from my faith in Christ. It is from this view I am able to judge my own sin. It would be most advantageous if our government would work in the same way. They would be conscience of the fact that most everything under their control is essentially ineffective and they would take necessary corrective measures to make a wrong, right. Since this is not the case, where our nation is headed is of great concern to me.

Within the ranks of common citizens, the pendulum has swung so far to the left that with parental approval, nine-year old female children are allowed to dress like ladies of the evening and mere boys are allowed to act like men. Out of control are criminal activity, child and spousal abuse, institutional corruption, criminal banking systems, compromised and failing educational systems, child pornography, negligence from our federal government whose duty is to protect our nation's borders, federal government chastising states that protect our borders at a time of obvious war with terrorists and illegal immigration, and corrupt inept political misrepresentatives with hip-shot solutions who view national hard times as opportunity. Opportunity for what is the question. Capping the irony of all this mêlée are governmental misrepresentatives who are paid large sums of money to make half-cocked decisions without accountability for failed out outcomes. And if an apology is in order, it should come from past and present leadership who have preyed upon the apathy and ignorance of America's citizenry. In the deepest sense, inept and corrupt leadership and liberal educators are much to blame for America's problems.

To make this book an equal playing field I also brought to light that Christians too, fall. The question is, when applying the principles tied to repentance we have to ask how much leeway should be allowed towards countless false promises of repentance, which is why to sin as a Christian is even worse. Even though the gospel saves, it also judges. Therefore, hiding behind the doctrine of salvation and grace does not justify continuance of inappropriate human indulgences. When, where, and how, does this vicious cycle stop? Without reservation I say that the social ills of society will never be cured as long as we continue to move the goal posts for levels of acceptance and tolerance, whether it is inside or outside the perimeters of Christian doctrine. By our own doing we are blaspheming the motto of "In God We Trust" and America as a whole is now facing the consequences of indictment on the charge of contributing to the tribulations of the last days. Philosophically, to me this says all systems have failed and the model for living is moving more and more towards deterioration without accountability. Biblically, I say that many of America's problems are because America has turned its back on God's grace: "I brought you into a bountiful country, to eat its fruit and its goodness. But when you entered, you defiled My land and made My heritage an abomination"[11]

The political and Christian views I have proposed throughout the book are quite bold. But in my opinion, they are timely. America's leadership and general populace have lost their fervor for recognizing the principalities of responsibility, accountability, and the God ordained moral and ethical ideals that gave America its strength. The total balance of these observations is summed up in the following brief synopsis:

The moral decay I speak of is not limited to deviant immoral sexual behavior. This moral decay is evidenced in how America does business in the service industry, real estate industry, stock exchange, governmental agencies, some churches, many of the once honorable professions, and most recent in the corruption found in the banking and mortgage industry. In one breath, we have a president who advocates that mothers return to school and in another breath he works to destroy the capitalist infrastructure of America. America has out-sourced most every aspect of her industrial might, while at the same time emphasizing the importance of why our children should attend school. Giving this set of circumstances it appears the logic behind attending school is more suitable for political indoctrination rather than a formal education that will eventually lead to the strength found in individualism. Christian values, the very heart of this great nation are under attack. Adding to America's decline, by virtue of habit alone, voters give into the falsities of party line loyalty and blindly vote for candidates, some of which quite frankly, should be jailed instead of exalted to positions of power. Having to pick from such a dishonorable lot is even more discouraging because it is obvious that neither political party is grounded in the specificities of their political past. They have become one and together actively pursue the reshaping of America in preparation for what I believe to be, the "New world Order." If there is one commonality political misrepresentative's share it's the abandonment of their duty to representing truth. Politicians do not understand the essence of truth because if they did, they would not do what they do conscionably. Americans have become like sheep whose hearts and minds have been numbed and corralled like complacent reserve park animals. While not all is lost, this is the most opportune time for the emergence of a strong independent political party whose ideals are entrenched in the conservative values that brought America to its greatness. Politicians and corporate CEO's exploit America's trust like a closed fraternity of wistful carpet- baggers. Who suffers the most from all this madness are the trusting people of good moral conscience. Once again, the context of truth has been revisited, misrepresented, and blasphemed by rogue and criminal characters in the night. It has been robed, chained, flogged, spat upon, and if you listen closely, you can hear the weight of the cross bouncing against the imperfections of the cobblestones.

In closing, if there is one common thread that runs throughout the book it is my love for Jesus Christ and His manual for living. There isn't anything in life that I can think of that supersedes His rational, purpose, warnings, and blessings. Undoubtedly, each chapter radiates this theme. Aside from expressing my own convictions relative to spiritual enlightenment, another one of my many goals was to present the idea that the light of Christ is for all to see and the key to living a redemptive life is not to wait for His light to come to you, you must go to it.

Without regret, now that I have addressed many of the things others might think but are too reluctant to say, it is time to reveal what I think is the only answer to the thesis question, can Christianity survive in a Godless nation?

My first inclination is that because of the magnitude of Christian fragmentation culminating from denominationalism, in conjunction with the various anti-Christian movements and government intervention, by definition the practicing rituals of Christianity as we know them may have difficulty surviving the internal and external vexatiousness that wounds the doctrinal structure and character of Christian belief. However, I am more confident that by the grace of God, these agencies will not cause the end of the spirit of Christianity because even living without faith in the almighty God housed in the wholesome eternal truths of the Holy Spirit, which is segued into the very word Christianity itself, Christian eternal survival is inevitable because the core essence of Christianity is directly and solely in and of Jesus Christ, not the government or its people. In the words of Julia Ward Howe, "As He died to make men holy, let us die to make men free."

Endnotes

About This Book
1   Ps.9:17 (KJV).
2   Isa.60:12.
3   Rev.22:19.
4   Matt.12:25.
5   Perry Stone, *Unleashing the Beast* (Lake Mary, Florida: Frontline Publishing, 2009), 142.

Introduction
1   Norman L. Geisler, *Christian Ethics: Options and Issues* (Grand Rapids, Michigan: Baker Bookhouse, 2004), 191.
2   Rev.22:18.
3   Isa. 40:25.
4   Isa. 40:18.
5   Ps. 132:13.
6   Stone, *Unleashing the Beast*, 130.
7   Isa. 33:22.
8   Isa.10:1.
9   Rom.2:12.
10 Isaiah 3:12.
11 J. Dwight Pentecost, Th.D., *Things to Come* (Grand Rapids, Michigan: Zondervan, 1964), 1.

Chapter One
1   Geisler, *Christian Ethics*, 32.
2   Ibid., 32-33.
3   Kevin J. Vanhoozer, *Is There A Meaning To This Text?* (Grand Rapids, Michigan, Zondervan, 1998), 39.
4   Deuteronomy 22:5.
5   Ezek. 7:9.
6   Rev. 22:7.

[7] Vanhoozer, Is There A Meaning To This Text?, 38.

[8] Jeremiah 10:12.

[9] Donald M. Broom, *The Evolution of Morality and Religion* (New York, New York: Cambridge University Press, 2003), 32.

[10] John 3:36.

[11] Norman L. Geisler, ed., *Inerrancy* (Grand Rapids, Michigan: Zodervan, 1984), 331.

[12] Pentecost, *Things to Come*, 269.

[13] Genesis 2:7.

[14] Stuart Hampshire, *Morality and Conflict* (Oxford, England: Basil Blackwell Publisher Limited, 1983), 19.

[15] Lewis B. Smeade, *Mere Morality-What God Expects from Ordinary People* (Grand Rapids, Michigan:William B. Eerdmans Publishing,1983),118.

[16] 2Tim. 4:3-4.

[17] Luke 21:36.

[18] John 14:6.

[19] John 14:14.

[20] Edward F. Hill, *The King James Version Defended*, Self-printing (1956), 2.

[21] Ibid. 2.

[22] Norman B. Harrison, *The End* (Minneapolis: Harrison Service, 1941), 87-88.

[23] Rom. 8:28.

[24] Geisler, *Inerrancy*, 17.

[25] Gen. 3:19.

[26] Arthur Pink, *Gleanings in Genesis* (Minneapolis: Filiquarian Publishing, LLC, 2006), 86.

[27] Rom.7: 14-15.

[28] Francis A. Schaeffer, *A Christian Manifested* (Westchester, Illinois: Crossway Publishing,1981), 100.

[29] Jerome M. Sattler, *Assessment of Children* (San Diego: San Diego State University, 1992), 70.

[30] Stuart Hampshire, *Morality and Conflict*, 21.

[31] Geisler, *Christian Ethics*, 191.

[32] Ibid., 88.

[33] Norman L. Geisler and J. Kirby Anderson, *Origin Science* (Grand Rapids, Michigan: Baker Books, 1987), 127-7.

[34] Geisler, *Christian Ethics*, 178.

[35] 1 Sam. 24:13.

[36] Broom, *The Evolution of Morality and Religion*, 137.

[37] Gen. 2:7.

[38] Geisler, *Inerrancy*, 66.

[39] Lev. 26:20.

[40] I Kings 11:36, 470.
[41] Stone, *Unleashing the Beast,* 130.
[42] Ibid., 84.
[43] John 8:14.

Chapter Two

[1] Stone, *Unleashing the Beast,* 141.
[2] 1Cor. 12:13.
[3] Timothy Ware, *The Orthodox Church* (Baltimore: Penguin Books, 1963), 51.
[4] 1Cor. 12:13.
[5] Acts 2:36.
[6] Alex Schemmann, *The Historical Road of Eastern Orthodoxy* (New York: Holt Rinehart and Winston, 1963), 34.
[7] Ibid., 35.
[8] John Meyendorff, *The Orthodox Church* (New York: Pantheon Books, 1962), 18.
[9] James H. Rutz, *The Open Church: How to Bring Back The Exciting Life of The First Century Church* (Beaumont, Texas: Seed Sowers, 1992), 55.
[10] Schemmann, *The Historical Road of Eastern* Orthodoxy, 69.
[11] Ibid., 70.
[12] Ibid., 71
[13] Ibid., 76.
[14] Ibid., 77.
[15] Earnest Benz, *The Eastern Orthodox Church* Chicago: Aldine Publishing Company, 1963), 166.
[16] Ibid.,164.
[17] Ware, *The Orthodox Church* 52.
[18] Col. 1:18.
[19] Ware, *The Orthodox Church,* 97.
[20] Ibid., 99.
[21] Ibid., *The Orthodox Church,* 154.
[22] Ibid., *The Orthodox Church,* 174.
[23] Ibid., 56.
[24] Ibid., 174.
[25] Gal. 3:28.
[26] Rutz, *The Open Church,* 58.
[27] Meyendorff, *The Orthodox Church,* 39.
[28] Ware, *The Orthodox Church,* 53.
[29] Ibid., 53.
[30] Ibid., 55.
[31] Meyendorff, *The Orthodox Church,* 32.
[32] Ibid., 33.

[33] Rutz, *The Open Church*, 13.

[34] Ibid.,110.

Chapter Three

[1] Richard Palmer, "What Really Happened in Bosnia," *Trumpet Magazine*, vol. 22, no. 7 (August 2011): 23.

[2] Ibid., 24.

[3] Dr. William P. Grady, *Final Authority* (Knoxville, Tennessee: Grady Publications Inc., 1993), 194.

[4] Edmond Paris, *Convert ... or Die!*, trans. Louis Perkins (Chino, California: Chick Publications), 59.

[5] Ibid., 130.

[6] Avro Manhattan, *The Vatican's Holocaust* (Springfield, Missouri: Ozark Books, 1982), 49.

[7] Ibid., 49.

[8] Paris, Convert...or Die!, 60.

[9] Ibid., 135.

[10] Manhattan, *The Vatican's Holocaust*, 48.

[11] Paris, *Convert ... or Die!*, 106.

[12] Edmond Paris, *The Vatican Against Europe*, trans. A. Robson (London: Wickliffe Press, 1961),209.

[13] Paris, *Convert ... or Die!*, 129.

[14] Ibid., 189.

[15] Manhattan, *The Vatican's Holocaust*, 33.

[16] Jasminka Udovicki and James Ridgeway, *Yugoslavia's Ethnic Nightmare* (New York: Lawrence Hill Publishers, 1995), 58.

[17] Noel Malcolm, *Bosnia: A Short History* (New York: New York University Press, 1994), 8.

[18] Mark Pinson, *The Muslims' of Herzegovina* (New York: New York University Press, 1994), 3.

[19] Malcolm, *Bosnia: A Short Story*, 11.

[20] Palmer, "What Really Happened in Bosnia," 24.

[21] Ibid., p. 22.

[22] Deut.16:19.

[23] Pinson, *The Muslims' of Herzegovina*, 23.

[24] Rabbi Yechiel Eckstein, President of Shoresh, *International Fellowship of Christians and Jews*, vol. 17, no. 7 (July, 2011).

[25] Malcolm, *Bosnia: A Short History*, 118.

[26] Udovicki and Ridgeway, *Yugoslavia's Ethnic Nightmare*, 3-4.

[27] Ibid., 1.

[28] Ibid., 4.

[29] Pinson, *The Muslims' of Herzegovina*, 141.

[30] Ibid., 144.

[31] Ibid., 144.

[32] Udovicki and Ridgeway, *Yugoslavia's Ethnic Nightmare*, 175.

[33] Ibid., 173.

[34] Ibid., 184.

[35] Palmer, "*What Really Happened in Bosnia*," 24.

[36] Ibid., 24.

[37] Udovicki and Ridgeway, *Yugoslavia's Ethnic Nightmare*, 184.

[38] Ibid., 189.

[39] Ibid., 190.

[40] Ibid., 190.

[41] Ibid., 191.

[42] John 8:32.

Chapter Four

[1] Matt. 24:6-9.

[2] Herbert Armstrong, *Mystery of the Ages* (Pasadena, California: World Wide Church of God, 1985), 166.

[3] Matt. 16:18.

[4] 2Tim. 4:3-4.

[5] Richard L. Niswonger, *New Testament History* (Grand Rapids, Michigan: Zondervan, 1988), 97.

[6] Albert Schweitzer, *Quest of The Historical Jesus* (Minneapolis: Fortress Press, 2001), 12.

[7] Vernon J. McGee, *Revelation Volume II* (Pasadena, California The Bible Books, 1984), 78.

[8] 2Tim. 3:16.

[9] Schweitzer, *Quest of The Historical Jesus*, 12.

[10] Heinz Zahrnt, *The Historical Jesus* (New York, New York: Harper and Row, 1963), 19.

[11] Gaalyah Cornfeld, ed., *The Historical Jesus* (New York: MacMillan Publishing, 1982), 13.

[12] Michael H. Burer, Th.M., Ph.D. *A Survey of Historical Jesus Studies: From Reimarus to Wright* (Bible.org, 2006), 2.

[13] Colin Tatum, *Quest of Historical Jesus* (Downers Grove, Illinois: Intervarsity Press, 1992), 326.

[14] Stanley Porter, *The Criteria for Authenticity in Historical Jesus Research* (Sheffield, England: Sheffield Academic Press, Ltd., 2000), 34.

[15] Martin Kahler, *The So-Called Jesus and The Historic Biblical Christ* (Philadelphia: Fortress Books, 1988), 46.

[16] Schweitzer, *Quest of the Historical Jesus*, 14.

[17] Raymond Martin, *The Elusive Messiah* (Boulder, Colorado: Westview Press, 1999), 29.

[18] Schweitzer, *Quest of The Historical Jesus*, 14.

[19] Eccl.1:9.

[20] W. Barnes Tatum, *In Quest of Jesus* (Nashville: Abingdon Press, 1999), 94.

[21] Ibid., 92.

[22] Ibid., 93.

[23] Ibid.

[24] Schweitzer, *Quest of The Historical Jesus*, 26.

[25] Wolfgang Stegman, Bruce J. Malina, and Gerd Theissen, *The Social Setting of Jesus and the Gospels.* (Minneapolis, Minnesota: Fortress Press), 2002),137.

[26] 2Tim. 3:16.

[27] G.A. Wells, *The Historical Evidence for Jesus* (Buffalo, New York: Prometheus Books, 1982), xi.

[28] John Warwick Montgomery, *Where is History Going?* (Newburg, Indiana. Trinity Press, 2001).186.

[29] Burer, *A Survey of Historical Jesus*, 2.

[30] Kahler, The So-Called Jesus and The Historical Christ, 46.

[31] Mal.3:1.

[32] Schweitzer, *Quest of the Historical Jesus*, 14.

[33] 2Tim. 1:13.

Chapter Five

[1] John Warwick Montgomery, *The Shaping of America* (Minneapolis: Bethany House Publishers, 1981), 123.

[2] Saint Theophan the Recluse, *Turning the Heart to God (*Ben Lemon, California: Conciliar Press, 2001), 9.

[3] Matt.5:48.

[4] CharlesE. Curran, *The Origins of Moral Theology in the United States* (Washington, D.C.: Georgetown University Press, 1997), 5.

[5] Stuart Hampshire, *Morality and Conflict* (Oxford, England: Basil Blackwell Publishers Limited, 1983), 29.

[6] Lewis B. Smedes, *Mere Morality-What God Expects from Ordinary People* (Grand Rapids, Michigan: Willard B. Eerdmans Publishing, 1983), 218.

[7] Hampshire, *Morality and Conflict*, 43.

[8] J.B. Shewing, ed., *Reason, Ethics, and Society* (Chicago: Cares Publishing Company, 1996), 42.

[9] B. Gert, *Morality: A New Justification of the Moral Rules (*New York: Oxford University Press, 1988), 47.

[10] Gilbert Ryle, *Conscience and Moral Convictions* (New York: Barnes and Noble, 1971), 185-193.

[11] Garth L. Harriett, *Christian Moral Reasoning – An Analytic Guide* (Notre Dame, Indiana: University of Notre Dame Press, 1983), 21.

[12] Russell Hardin, *Morality with Limits of Reason* (Chicago: University of Chicago Press, 1998), 4.

[13] Ezek.,7:3.
[14] Rom. 1:1, 15:27; 1 Cor. 10:3, 15:4, Eph. 1:3. 5:19.
[15] Job 8:1.
[16] John 6:63.
[17] Matt.6:21.
[18] Margaret C. Jasper, *The Right To Die* (New York: Oceana Publications, 2000).
[19] Ibid., 40.
[20] Ibid.,7.
[21] Ibid., 9.
[22] Daniel Hilliard and John Dombrink, *Dying Right* (New York: Rutledge Press, 2000), 9.
[23] Jasper, *The Right To Die*, p.8.
[24] "Ethics and Law: Physician Assisted Dying," *Journal of Palliative Medicine* 8, no. 3 (2005): 611.
[25] "Passive Euthanasia", *Journal of Medical Ethics*, no. 21, (2005).
[26] Ibid., 65.
[27] "Ethics and Law: Physician Assisted Dying," 609.
[28] Ibid., 609.
[29] Waldo Beach, *Christian Ethics of the Protestant Tradition* (Atlanta: John Knox Press, 1988), 74.
[30] James Haley, *Death and Dying* (Farmington Hills, Minnesota: Green Haven Press, 2003), 7.
[31] "Ethics and Law: Physician Assisted Dying,"611.
[32] "The Challenge of Terri Schiavo: Lessons for Bioethics," *Journal of Medical Ethics* (2005): 376.
[33] Ibid., 376.
[34] "Ethics in Law: Physician Assisted Dying,"609.
[35] Jasper, *The Right To Die*, 20.
[36] Ibid., 1.
[37] Cleverest Koop, *The Memories of America's Family Doctor*, 1991.
[38] "Are Attempts to Have Impaired Children Justifiable?" *Journal of Medical Ethics*, no. 28. (2002):5.
[39] "Ethics, Law, and the Assisted Reproductive Technology," *Journal of Ethics and Behavior* 6, no. 4 (1996):369.
[40] R.D. Orr and M. Siegler, "Ethical Issues Involved in Posthumous Sperm Retrieval," *Family Weekly* (December 9, 2002), 11.
[41] 2Timothy 3:2-7, 1483.
[42] Montgomery, *The Shaping of America*, 181.
[43] Ibid., 181.

Chapter Six

[1] Job 8:13.
[2] John 6:63.

Matthew 6:21.

[3] Matthew 6:21.
[4] Proverbs 22:6.
[5] Matthew 7:15.
[6] R. L. Bruckberger, *Image of America*, Catholic Hour din, 1959, q. v.
[7] Rom.1:28.
[8] 1Cor. 2:14.
[9] Eccl. 3:1.
[10] Ps. 103:3.
[11] Ex. 2:23.
[12] Gen. 1:29.
[13] Isa. 44:10.
[14] Gen. 3:21.
[15] Ibid., 1:26.
[16] Ibid., 6:18.
[17] Ibid., 8:21.
[18] Matt. 16:24.
[19] Ibid., 6:33.
[20] 1Peter 4:18.
[21] Geisler, *Christian Ethics*, 232.
[22] Jeremiah 17:9.
[23] Mark 3:24.
[24] Matthew 7:15.
[25] John 5:19.
[26] Mark 13:22.
[27] Romans 14:12

Epilogue

[1] 2Corinthians 11:13.
[2] 2Timothy 3:5.
[3] 2Corinthians 2:5.
[4] I John 3:3.
[5] I John 4:3.
[6] Ecclesiastes 12:14.
[7] John 14: 6-7.
[8] Ibid., 12:48.
[9] Psalm 14:1.
[10] John 8:47.
[11] Jeremiah 2:7

110

Bibliography

Allen, Joseph, and Michael Najim, Jack Sparks, and Theodore Stylianopoulos. *The Orthodox Study Bible-New Testament and Psalms*, Nashville, Tennessee: Nelson Publishers, 1979.

Armstrong, Herbert. *Mystery of the Ages*. Pasadena, California: Worldwide Church of God, 1985.

Beach, Waldo. *Christian Ethics of the Protestant Tradition*. Atlanta, Georgia: John Knox Publishing, 1988.

Benz, Earnest. *The Orthodox Church*. Chicago, Illinois: Aldine Publishing Company, 1963.

Bradley, James E. and Richard Mueller. *Church History-An Introduction to Research, Reference Works, and Methods.* Grand Rapids, Michigan: William B. Eerdmans Publishing Company, 1995.

Bray, Gerald. *Biblical Interpretation-Past and Present.* Downers Grove, Illinois: Intervarsity Press, 1996.

Broom, Donald M. *The Evolution of Morality and Religion.* Cambridge, United Kingdom, University Press, 2003.

Bruckberger, R.L. *Image of America*. Trans. by C.G. Paulding and V. Peterson. New York, New York: Viking, 1959.

Burer, Michael H. *A Survey of Historical Jesus Studies: From Reimarus to Wright.* www.bible.org, 2006.

Cornfield, Galyak, ed. *The Historical Jesus*. New York and London: Macmillan Publishing, 1963.

Curran, Charles E. *The Origins of Moral Theology in the United States.* Washington D.C,: Georgetown University Press, 1997.

Eckstein, Yechiel and Rabbi Shoresh. *International Fellowship of Christians and Jews* 17, <u>no.</u> 7 (July 2011).

Flurry, Gerald, ed. *What Really Happened in Bosnia* 22, <u>no.</u> 7 (2011).

Geisler, Norman L. *Christian Ethics and Options and Issues.* Grand Rapids, Michigan: Baker Bookhouse, 2004.

Geisler, Norman L., ed. *Inerrancy.* Grand Rapids, Michigan: Zondervan Publishing House, 1984.

Geisler, Norman L. and Anderson, J. Kirby. *Origin Science.* Grand Rapids, Michigan: Baker House, 1987, 127-57.

Gert, B. *Morality: A New Justification of the Moral Rules.* New York, New York: Oxford University Press, 1988.

Grady, Dr. William P. *Final Authority.* Knoxville, Tennessee: Grady Publications, Inc., 1993.

Gundry, Robert H. *A Survey of the New Testament, 4th ed.* Grand Rapids, Michigan: Zondervan, 2003.

Guthrie, Donald. *New Testament Introduction, 4th ed.* Downers Grove, Illinois: Intervarsity Press, 1990.

Hampshire, Stuart. *Morality and Conflict.* Oxford, England: Basil Blackwell Publisher Limited, 1983.

Hardin, Russell. *Morality with Limits and Reason.* Illinois, Chicago and London: University Press of Chicago, 1983.

Harriet, Garth L. *Christian Moral Reasoning –An Analytic Guide.* Notre Dame, Indiana: University of Notre Dame Press, 1983.

Harrison, Norman B., *The End*. Minnesota: Harrison Service, 1941.

Hill, Edward. *The King James Version Defended*. Self Published, 1956.

Hilliard, Daniel and John Dombrink. *Dying Right*. New York, New York: Rutledge Press, 2000.

Hearth, Alfred J., Gerald L. Mattingly, and Edwin M. Yamauchi. *Peoples of the Old Testament World*. Grand Rapids, Michigan: Baker Books, 1998.

Hopfe, Lewis M. *Religions of the World*, 6th ed. Englewood Cliffs, New Jersey: Prentice Hall, 1994.

Jasper, Margaret C. *The Right to Die*. Dobbs Ferry, New York: Oceana Press, 2000.

"Are Attempts to Have Impaired Children Justifiable? Journal of Medical Ethics, no. 28 (2002).

"Ethics, Law, and the Assisted Reproductive Technologies." Journal of Ethics, Law, and Behavior 6, no. 4 (1996): 368.

"The Challenge of Terri Schiavo: Lessons in Bioethics." Journal of Medical Ethics (2005).

Journal of Palliative Medicine 8, no. 3 (2005).

"*Passive Euthanasia.*" Journal of Medical Ethics, no. 21 (2005).

Kahler, Martin. *The So-Called Jesus and the Historical Bible Christ*. Philadelphia, Pennsylvania: Fortress Books, 1988.

Koop, Everett C. *The Memories of America's Family Doctor.* 1991.

Malcolm, Noel. *Bosnia-A Short History*. New York: New York University Press, 1994.

Manhattan, Avro. *The Vatican's Holocaust*. Springfield, Missouri: Ozark Books, 1986.

Martin, Raymond. *The Elusive Messiah*. Boulder, Colorado:Westview Press, 1999.

Matera, Frank J. *New Testament Ethics - The Legacies of Jesus and Paul*. Louisville, Kentucky: Westminster John Knox Press, 1996.

McGee, Vernon J. *Revelation Volume I*. Pasadena, California: The Bible Books, 1984.

McRay, John. *Archaeology and the New Testament*, 2nd ed. Grand Rapids, Michigan: Baker Academic, 1991.

Meyendorff, John. *The Orthodox Church*. USA: Pantheon Books, 1962.

Michael, St. Archangel. *Church Bulletin*. Illinois, Chicago: Serbian Eastern Orthodox Church, Monthly.

Montgomery, John Warwick. *The Shaping of America*. Minneapolis, Minnesota: Bethany Howe Publishers, 1981.

Montgomery, John Warwick. *Where is History Going?* Newburg, Indiana: Trinity Press, 2001.

Niswonger, Richard L. *New Testament History*. Grand Rapids, Michigan: Zondervan Publishing House, 1988.

Orr, R.D. and M. Siegler. "Ethical Issues Involved in Posthumous Sperm Retrieval." *Family Weekly* (2002).

Osborne, Grant R. *The Hermeneutical Spiral*. Downers Grove, Illinois: Intervarsity Press, 1991.

Paris, Edmond. *Convert ... or Die!* Chino, California: Chick Publications, n.d.

Paris, Edmond. *The Vatican Against Europe*. Wickliffe Press: London, 1961.

Pentecost, Dwight J. *Things to Come*. Grand Rapids, Michigan: Zondervan, 1964.

Pinson, Mark. *The Muslims of Herzegovin*. New York: New York University Press, 1994.

Porter, Stanley. *The Criteria for Authenticity in Historical Jesus Research*. England: Sheffield Academic Press, LTD, 2000.

Pretzel, Calvin J. *The World That Shaped the New Testament*. Atlanta, Georgia: John Knox Press, 1985.

Rutz, James H. *The Open Church-How to Bring Back the Exciting Life of the First Century Church*. Beaumont, Texas: Seed Growers Publishing, 1992.

Ryle, Gilbert. *Conscience and Moral Convictions*. New York, New York: Barnes and Noble, 1971.

Sattler, Jerome M. *Assessment of Children*. San Diego, California: San Diego State University, 1992.

Schaeffer, Francis A. *A Christian Manifested*. Westchester, Illinois: Crossway Publishing, 1981.

Schemmann, Alex. *The Historical Road of Eastern Orthodoxy*. New York: Holt, Rinehart, and Winston, 1963.

Schneewind, J.B., ed. *Reason, Ethics, and Society*. Chicago and LaSalle, Illinois: Carus Publishing Company, 1996.

Schweitzer, Albert. *Quest of the Historical Jesus*. Minneapolis, Minnesota: Fortress Press, Reprint, 2001.

Smeade, Lewis B. *Mere Morality-What God Expects from Ordinary People*. Grand Rapids, Michigan: William Eerdsman Publishing, 1983.

Sproul, R.C. and John Gerstner, and Arthur Lindsley. *Classical Apologetics*. Grand Rapids, Michigan: Zondervan Publishing House, 1984.

Stegman, Wolfgang, Malina, Bruce J., and Theissen,Gerd. *The Social Setting of Jesus and the Gospels*. Minneapolis, Minnesota: Fortress Press, 2002.

Stone, Perry. *Unleashing the Beast*. Lake Mary, Florida: Frontline Publishing, 2011.

Schweitzer, Albert. *Quest of the Historical Jesus*. Minneapolis, Minnesota: Fortress Press, Reprint 2001.

Stegman, Wolfgang and Molina, Bruce. *The Social Setting of Jesus and the Gospels. Minneapolis, Minnesota*: Fortress Press, 2002.

Tatum, W. Barnes. *In Quest of Jesus*. Nashville, Tennessee: Abingdon Press, 1999.

Theophan, St. The Recluse. *Turning the Heart to God*. Ben Lomond, California: Conciliar Press, 2001.

Udovicki, Jaminka, and James Ridgeway. *Yugoslavia's Ethnic Nightmare*. New York, New York: Lawrence Hill Publishing, 1995.

Vanhoozer, Kevin J. *Is There a Meaning to This Text?* Grand Rapids, Michigan: Zondervan, 1998.

Ware, Timothy. *The Orthodox Church*. Baltimore, Maryland: Penguin Books, 1963.

Wells, G.A. *The Historical Evidence for Jesus*. Buffalo, New York: Prometheus Books, 1982.

Zahrnt, Heinz. *The Historical Jesus*. New York, New York: Harper and Row, 1963.